The Good Death Guide

Inspiring, informative books for thoughtful readers wanting to make changes and realise their potential.

Other **Pathways** books include:

Building Your Life Skills
Who are you, where are you, and where do
you want to go: a personal action plan

Choosing a Better Life
An inspiring step-by-step guide to
building the future you want

When What You've Got Is Not What You Want
Use NLP to create the life you want
and live it to the full

Healing the Hurt Within
Understand and relieve the suffering
behind self-destructive behaviour

Please send for a free copy of the catalogue for full details
(see back cover for address).

The Good Death
Guide

*Everything you wanted to know
but were afraid to ask*

Michael Dunn

PATHWAYS

First published in 2000 by
How To Books Ltd, 3 Newtec Place,
Magdalen Road, Oxford OX4 1RE, United Kingdom
Tel: 01865 793806 Fax: 01865 248780

British Library Cataloguing in Publication Data
A catalogue record for this book is available from
the British Library

Editing by Julie Nelson / Cover image PhotoDisc
Cover design by Shireen Nathoo Design

Produced for How To Books by Deer Park Productions
Typeset by PDQ Typesetting, Stoke-on-Trent, Staffs.
Printed and bound in Great Britain

Note: The material contained in this book is set out in good
faith for general guidance and no liability can be accepted for
loss or expenses incurred as a result of relying in particular
circumstances on statements made in the book. The laws and
regulations are complex and liable to change, and readers
should check the current position with the relevant
authorities before making personal arrangements.

Pathways is an imprint of
How To Books

Contents

Preface   ix

1 Facts and attitudes   1
Why are we born? Why should we die?   2
The ageing process   7
Fear of dying   14
But what about the pain?   19
More people used to be born – and died young   23
The place where we die has changed   24
Death language   27

2 When will you die?   29
What will be the cause of your death?   35
It's worse for men   37
How long would you *like* to live?   39
There are ways of living for ever   40
A good death   44
How can we lengthen our life span?   46

3 Getting down to it   61
Making your will   61
Donating your organs after death   64
Donating your body for research   67
Advance directives: living wills   68
The anticipated death   72
How long have I got, doctor?   78
But he mustn't be told...   79
The near death experience   82
Your deathbed scene   84
But I was speaking to her only this morning...   88
Hospice care   89
Assisted death   93
Involuntary assisted death   99

4 The day itself has arrived   104
   The physical process of dying   104
   Laying-out and preparing a body   110
   Registering the death   111
   Post-mortems   116

5 Arranging a funeral   119
   The funeral director   119
   How do they know what to do?   123
   How much will a funeral cost?   124
   How to get ahead in funeral directing   127
   Who pays for the funeral?   128
   Pre-purchased funerals   129
   What if you are dissatisfied with your funeral director?   133
   Embalming and preparation   133

6 Disposal of the body   138
   Burial   139
   Cremation   141
   Gravestones and memorials   147
   Sorting out the estate   148
   Welfare benefits following a death   151

7 Home organised funerals   154
   Doing it yourself   154
   Home burials and cremations   164
   Woodland burials   165
   Organising a secular funeral   165

8 After the funeral has passed   175
   Bereavement   175
   Attachment   177
   How to have closer relationships with reduced attachment   178
   The physical damage that grief can cause   181
   It's not, however, all doom and gloom   182
   How to be bereaved successfully   183
   The more subtle injuries of grief   185
   Grief opportunities   186
   Helping bereaved people   187

9   **Different deaths**   191
    The death of a parent   191
    The death of a child   193
    Miscarriage, stillbirth and baby death   196
    Suicide   197
    Death in other cultures   200
    Death and homosexuality   201
    HIV/AIDS and death   202
    Burial at sea   204
    Pets and death   206
    Best behaviour   207
    In conclusion   211

10 **Telegrams from the grave**   216

Appendixes
    I   Public opinion about assisted death   221
    II   Laying-out a body   223
    III   Funeral costs by UK region   225
    IV   Checklist of things to be done after a death   227
    V   Making your own coffin   229
    VI   Further reading   231
    VII   Death on the Internet   233

    Index   *237*

Acknowledgements

I would like to thank all who helped in the research of this book, in particular, Wendy Gaywood, Suzanne Helm, Dr Peter Leedham, Margaret Pillsbury, Mark Ratcliffe, Shrewsbury Crematorium, Shropshire Libraries, Dudley Summerskill, Ken West and, especially, Rita.

Preface

We shall not cease from exploration
And the end of all our exploring
Will be to arrive where we started
And know the place for the first time.

T. S. Eliot, *The Four Quartets*

There is a lot of literature about dying. Most of it is about dealing with the shocked aftermath of someone's death – first aid for survivors. There are many moving accounts – usually by widows – of how people recovered and 'came to terms' with the death of a loved one; these deaths usually came unexpectedly and the survivors found themselves stranded in a new and unfamiliar world. There are other books with titles like *What to do...*, *Where to get help...*, *How to help bereaved people....*

We usually only begin to think and talk about death when a terminal disease is confirmed – leaving only a short time to face the reality, make arrangements and overcome inhibitions, anxieties and fears that have been established over a lifetime.

Mostly we know next to nothing about the facts of the physical process of death, what a funeral director does or what choices we have about burial or cremation: we pay handsomely for others to protect us from such 'unsavoury' details.

We almost consciously refuse to imagine what changes in our lives would follow the deaths of partners, friends, parents and children: we are taught that such thinking is morbid and unhealthy – there is even a feeling that just thinking about death may be sufficient to bring it about. We almost cultivate our ignorance and lack of preparation as though it is *desirable* that they should be added to our grief to sharpen it.

Underlying our refusal to come to grips with the subject is the lingering knowledge from infancy that we are special: life will get better and better. In the context of continual improvement, death is nonsense: an obscenity.

However, we all know that death will come eventually. We can't hold these two conflicting ideas together in our mind so we simply pretend that death will not happen to us and our loved ones.

If we refer to death, our own or others, we are likely to be rebuked: 'Don't be morbid', 'Don't talk like that', 'Nonsense, you'll outlive us all'. Just because most people take this attitude, doesn't mean that it's mature, healthy or wise.

I remember when I was working as a social worker some years ago in Cumbria: I knew a family then who were in the midst of death.

The mother, Sue, (none of these names are real) had been separated from Robert for a year and was just settling into her life as a single mother on state benefits. Her son Jamie had just started school and Sue was thinking about how she might get back into teaching. The future looked bright but, that February, she was told she had cancer: a virulent, advanced catastrophe that would see her dead by Christmas.

It wasn't as clear as that at the beginning. There was a 70 per cent chance of successful treatment, but if it didn't work – and she had to force this out of the hospital – she had between six months and two years to live.

For two days she lived alone with this in disbelief. She'd always been an optimist in times of trouble and she looked for hope where she could. But it was going to be hard to squeeze any silver lining out of this.

So she decided that she simply would not believe the doctors. She felt well: 'she did not have cancer'. She allowed herself a few hours indignation about misdiagnosis before gradually giving up the pretence.

The first person she told was Jamie's teacher who found her quietly weeping in the playground. Miss Richardson took her into the classroom, made her a cup of coffee, and told her about a friend who had the same thing and was back on her feet again.

The next person to know was her brother, Peter. They had never been particularly close but he could be depended upon to keep a level head. She dreaded her mother finding out – Mum would go to pieces: Sue couldn't cope with that as well.

And then there was Robert: as Jamie's father he would have

to be told. Peter went to see him and his new partner. Robert was devastated but Peter could see that he was confused about how to respond. He had left Sue for Diane and her children and had only seen Jamie a couple of times since the bitter departure a year ago. There had been no divorce – he remained Sue's husband. He wondered what responsibility people in his position should have.

He went to see Sue the following day. He tried out lines from similar situations but they jarred painfully: 'I can't tell you how sorry I am'; 'You look well'; 'Let me know if there's anything I can do – anything at all'; 'I do hope you'll feel better'. They ended positively: they mustn't give up hope – the radiation treatment was going to be successful. Then Robert went home to Diane. Diane asked (a little anxiously) what would happen to Jamie 'if anything should happen to Sue'.

Peter couldn't have visited her at a worse time a few weeks later. Sue was depressed after one of her treatments and directed her misery at him: she dragged up childhood incidents where he had been cruel and unprotective: how he had always been their mother's favourite. There was a row and, feathers ruffled, Peter left with a parting remark about 'not being appreciated'.

Robert telephoned every week but showed no increased interest in Jamie: he did, however, become more regular in his financial support, sometimes even sending extra.

It wasn't long before Peter told their mother, who turned up in tears, upset at being the last to know. She was full of advice: she should have a second opinion; she should be much more assertive about finding more information; she would 'have to put on a brave front' if Jamie wasn't to be upset.

Weeks passed. By now Sue was beginning increasingly to feel the effects of the treatments; she was also beginning to look ill. She was losing weight and becoming more and more depressed. Her GP gave her some tablets, which made her lethargic. She tired easily: her mother decided to move in and took over the housekeeping and the care of Jamie.

The consultant's hinted news that the treatment wasn't working was a trigger for Sue's hidden anxieties and terrors to erupt. She became obsessed with becoming cured. Within a few weeks she had spent her £2,500 savings on alternative treatments: to no effect.

She became convinced – for no reason – that exercise was the answer. She would be gone for long periods – walking around to the point of exhaustion. Nobody who knew her could understand her attitude to Jamie: she seemed icily indifferent to him. Her mother colluded by keeping him apart from Sue as much as possible ('Mummy will be better soon'). Part of Sue welcomed this separation – she just couldn't cope with the idea of death taking her away from her son.

Things became worse. She had no energy and a lot of pain; she lost her appetite and retreated, miserable, into herself. She resented her mother's relationship with Jamie – just like with Peter when they were children.

Her mother made it clear that 'if the worst come to the worst, there'll always be a home with me for Jamie.' Jamie was becoming impatient about Sue not getting better. Robert and Peter kept away – pleased that Sue had her mother to care for her.

The pain became unbearable: her GP increased the drugs – 'You'll feel sleepy...'. Sue lost most of her awareness of her surroundings three days before she died. By now her appearance was shocking. She had been admitted to hospital and her mother had moved back home with Jamie. Sue died alone during the night.

After the funeral everybody said how brave she had been. Not only Sue – hadn't Jamie taken it well? They all wished they'd had the opportunity to tell her how much she had meant to them. But 'it had all been so unexpected.' Everyone was devastated: but this was not thought unusual – after all, bereavement is always a painful business.

Usually this is the point where the books on dealing with death start.

However, if we look more closely at the hurt and pain of all concerned – including Sue – we shall discover that much of it could have been diminished if there had been greater openness and preparation.

This had been the pathetic fading away of a terrified, drugged, 'failed' mother – leaving behind guilty, emotionally scarred survivors. In other circumstances, it could have been the dignified but regretted completion of the life of a fondly remembered woman – a miserably sad occasion, but one that had been achieved peacefully and painlessly: nothing would have been left unsaid and the future could have been positive and less distressing for the survivors.

We can only live our life fully if we take the fact of our death into account. This will affect our aims in life, decisions we make, relationships with others and management of our resources: it will determine the very meaning that we attach to life itself.

The aims of this book are:

◆ To try to unravel and explain our horror of death.
◆ To consider the whys, wheres, whens and hows of death.
◆ To look at how we can change our life to gain optimum longevity.
◆ To imagine the circumstances of our death and plan to influence them.
◆ To show the range of choice about funeral arrangements and how we can take some responsibility for our own.
◆ To give information about the funeral business and how to make best use of a funeral director.
◆ To take a hard, factual look at the processes of dying, last offices, embalming, cremation and burial.
◆ To look at the consequences for others of different sorts of death.
◆ To describe bereavement and how preparation earlier in relationships can reduce its sharpness.

By opening up this book and getting this far, you are on the way to changing the way you live your life and the way you will experience not only the deaths of others but also your own.

Michael Dunn

As I am now,
so you must be:
Therefore
prepare to
follow me.
MEMORIAL,
WOOLWICH

CHAPTER 1

Facts and Attitudes

D eath is very unpopular. When you think about the other
major landmarks in life, death is badly represented.
Being born, getting christened, getting married, giving birth,
getting qualified, birthdays, retirement – these are times to be
anticipated, acknowledged and celebrated: they mark our
changing relationship with others.

They are planned stops in the progress of our life stories
when we can mark important changes in the shape of our
development. There is a continuing sense of moving forward
positively, gathering knowledge and experience.

To a greater or lesser extent, we have some destination in
mind. We look forward to things improving: we can imagine
some vague distant future when we can look back with
satisfaction on a life well-lived. There will be a sense of
fulfilment – all the loose ends will be tied up: our life will be
complete.

However, what should be the climax of our living so often
takes places offstage in an anxious, unplanned, muddled way
that puts us to shame. We seem to be bad at taking our deaths
seriously. If we talk about death at all, we are embarrassed and
lost for words; our imagination becomes resistant.

We conspire between us to maintain this attitude (or,
rather, *lack* of attitude). To spend time thinking about death is
seen as morbid, unnatural and unhealthy: there is a suspected
implication of brooding on anticipated suicide. Dying has
become almost exclusively associated with disease and medical
matters, where it is regarded as 'failure'.

Our perceptions of ourselves are heavily influenced by
printed and electronic media which choose to promote youth
and glamour: death and its associations with older people have
no place here. In this way older people have been set aside so
that the rest of us can avoid facing up to our mortality.

Why are we born? Why should we die?

> *Coeval with the first pulsation, when the fibres quiver, and the*
> *organs quiver into vitality, is the germ of death. Before our*
> *members are fashioned, is the narrow grave dug, in which they*
> *are to be entombed.*
>
> Sir A. Palgrave, *Merchant and Friar*

Before going any further, it's worth considering nothing less
than the whole meaning of life. Why are we here? What's the
point of death?

Your guess is as good as mine. However, some people's
guesses are rather better. Let's look at some of the ideas that
have been suggested which are relevant to our understanding.

A genetic argument

In his book *The Selfish Gene*, Richard Dawkins sets out a
startling view of the meaning of life. Where philosophers and
psychologists flatter our sense of importance as individuals
living fulfilled lives in communities, he describes us as *survival
machines*. We have been developed genetically over generations
to act as hosts for the genes of our ancestors. Our genes will
keep us functioning efficiently so that we can find a likely
partner who may be able to introduce some fresh, interesting
genetic material to our own genes. In this way we can produce
baby 'survival machines' which will, if all goes well, be
genetically improved. They can then continue the process.

Our genes are only interested in us as forms of transport to
the next generation. After a certain age there is a drop in the
quality of our genetic material, so we are programmed to have
children during the first half of our lives. After that we're not
much use to our genes so they lose interest and being to 'fail'.
They're in charge, we've posted off copies of them to our
children, there's nothing more to do...we die.

This is an elegant and convincing – if bleak and humbling
– explanation of existence: it puts us in our place and
challenges our self-importance. Can we accept that we are not
as 'in charge' as we thought – that life is personally
meaningless? We may have to concentrate more on what we
can experience and give to others now rather than anticipating
dreams for the future.

This is not to say that our lives are over when we have had children. Older people, even though they can no longer play a successful part in passing on genetic material, can continue to influence their children and grandchildren with their knowledge and experience. Similarly, other people who do not have children can make their mark on others during their lifetimes.

These 'influences' Richard Dawkins calls 'memes' (pronounced 'meemes'). They are, for example, the cultural or religious ideas, myths, behaviour, habits, political ideas, music or fairy tales which are passed on and developed from generation to generation and help define our common culture and humanity. A powerful example is family memories, which give us our biographies and are passed on with suitable amendments (just like genes) to future generations.

However, the gene remains in charge and will choose to adapt to our ideas only if it falls in with its own selfish ends: after our child-bearing years are over, we're on our own:

> *(The gene) leaps from body to body down the generations, manipulating body after body in its own way and for its own ends, abandoning a succession of mortal bodies before they sink in senility and death.... When we have served our purpose we are cast aside. But genes are denizens of geological time.... Genes, like diamonds, are forever.*
>
> Richard Dawkins, *The Selfish Gene*

Richard Dawkins accounts for the menopause as a gene decision to shut down a woman's failing childbirth equipment so that her energy can be more fruitfully invested in support of her grown-up children and grandchildren.

We *could* increase our life spans. Imagine if everyone were forty before they were allowed to have children: eventually our genes (which are only interested in being reproduced) would begin to reject those of us who couldn't manage delayed parenthood. We could gradually raise the age at which reproduction was allowed until we achieved a genetically developed populated of young, 100–year-old parents who completed their lives after two or three centuries.

This would probably be an entirely feasible project.

However, the emphasis would be on the extension of our physical existence. It begs the question of how our psychological selves or the world economy would cope with it.

We seem at present to 'pace' our mental life to run happily alongside our present physical life span. We note that older people often seem to develop an acceptance of their forthcoming deaths: sometimes there is depression or disease behind this, but there does seem to be a feeling in the seventies, eighties or nineties that our lives are nearing completion and that death will be a fitting outcome. It's not that we want to die: death becomes 'appropriate'.

> *Make way for others, as others have done for you.*
>
> Montaigne, French philosopher

> *If all creatures were immortal and preserved the same functions and abilities through their endless lives, they would pre-empt the possibility of improvement or adaptation.... In the absence of senescence and death, these young hopefuls would enter an overcrowded stage. By modest withdrawal from the scene, one generation acknowledges and gives way to the unforeseeable talents of the next.*
>
> Jonathan Miller, *The Body in Question*, Jonathan Cape 1978

An ecological argument

> *The present population of Latin America is around 300 million, and already many of them are undernourished. But if the population continued to increase at the present rate, it would take less than 500 years to reach the point where people, packed in a standing position, formed a solid human carpet over the whole area of the continent.... In 1,000 years from now they would be standing on each others' shoulders more than a million deep. By 2,000 years, the mountain of people, travelling outwards at the speed of light, would have reached the edge of the known universe.*
>
> Richard Dawkins, *The Selfish Gene*

That won't happen, of course: either the birth rate will decline or the death rate will increase – or both; there just wouldn't be enough food to go around. Certainly, there is no question of extending the life span. Our deaths are essential.

In some publicity issued by London Zoo, it was stated that there is a type of aphid which is very short-lived: it dies after a few days. In order to maintain a population capable of surviving, it produces many baby aphids. It is essential that there is a balance between the early death of the parent and the number of young produced. If there were no balance and a pair of aphids could – only theoretically, thank goodness – live for twelve months there would be chaos: they could be responsible for a layer of relatives covering the whole surface of the earth to a thickness of 93 miles.

> *In 1960 the world's population was three billion. Around a year from now it will reach twice that figure. There are nearly as many human beings alive on the planet today as ever lived on it up to the start of this (twentieth) century. Soon, for the first time in history, the ancient Greek catchword for death – 'joining the majority' – will cease to be accurate.*
>
> John Gray, *The Guardian*, August 1998

A biological perspective

> *One is hard put to stop being dead.*
>
> M. M. Pardi

The Volvo is a wonderful car: it's reliable, it has stamina and it will survive rough treatment and accident damage. On the other hand, it's heavy, it's unsporty and it will never win a Grand Prix. The MG is also a wonderful car: it's fast, responsive, exciting and easily manoeuvrable. However, it won't survive 200,000 miles of hard driving and it's definitely not somewhere to be in a head-on crash. Neither car, however, was built to be something it is not. What you get is what you want.

It's the same with the body: it's built for a purpose. We may all have our own opinions about why we're here, but our body's biological purpose, as we have seen, is dominated by the needs of those arrogant little genes.

We may think that the purpose of life is to do with self-fulfilment and the gaining of wisdom – and those may be good things to do in our spare time – but there's nothing in it for the genes. As far as they're concerned, we've established their next generation. All the genetic energy, therefore, is focused on sustaining us during the early and middle years of life.

There could have been another choice for the genes. They could have organised things so that we combined longevity with fertility: we could have lived to 200 years with 100 years in the middle for producing 20 children. However, the extra biological and psychological equipment we would need would have been so cumbersome and 'costly' that it wouldn't have been worth it.

If all you want is to be passed on to make as many good new gene connections as you can, it's obviously been decided genetically that lots of fresh, quickly succeeding generations provide the best environment.

To go back to the car comparison, it would be possible to build a vehicle that had the durability, stamina and safety features of a Volvo and the speed and sportiness of an MG but it would probably have to be jet-powered and the size of a large truck. It would be costly on resources, unmarketable and unfriendly to the High Street.

So the genes had a choice: we could be short-lived, fertile and cheap or very old, fertile and very expensive. The market forces of genetics prefer a bargain. So we're stuck with our three score years and ten – and a few more if we're lucky.

This is not to say that we are 'programmed' to die. It's just that there's been no effort put into making our bodies longer-lived. After middle age our cells and organs are on their own. The material from which our body cells are constructed becomes less efficient at its job: in particular our staple diet – oxygen – can begin to have a toxic effect on cell metabolism leaving them vulnerable to cancer development and other nasty outcomes.

Old age is seldom seen in most animals: when a gazelle gets a touch of arthritis it can't run as fast and it gets eaten. It has been said that no one has seen a bear in the wild which had died of natural causes.

It's only with human beings that old age can regularly be sustained by greater health awareness, medical care and social and family support. This can lead to 'bonus' years denied to our ancestors; it can also bring about situations – as we shall see – where we begin to think that we are being kept alive longer than is appropriate.

What happens, then, to cause us to decline?

The ageing process

AS SOON AS WE TO BE BEGUNNE
WE DID BEGINNE TO BE UNDONE

English Memento Mori Medal, c.1650

How long should we live? An accepted formula for calculating this, in mammals, is based on the multiplication by five of the time it takes the skeleton to mature. Thus, because a dog's growing period is three years, its life span average is considered to be fifteen years. Human skeletal growth is complete by the age of 25 and, so, a fair estimate of our life expectancy is around 120 to 125 years. Anyone failing to get close to this is losing a good number of potentially happy and productive years.

Leon Chaitow, *The Ageing Process*

We start to die almost from the moment of conception as cells are destroyed to shape our bodies. Most of our cells are constantly being replaced – for example, during our lifetime we lose about 18 kg of skin. Various parts of us reach their peak performance as we proceed through life:

- ◆ 10 years old: our hearing is at its peak.
- ◆ 20 years old: our visual acuity is sharpest.
- ◆ 30 years old: the peak for muscular strength, speed and accuracy of co-ordination.
- ◆ 40 years old: heart and blood vessels begin to deteriorate.
- ◆ 50 years old: learning ability slows, emotional reactions become flatter, imagination weakens – as does the capacity for fresh creative thinking.

Nobody dies of old age. What happens is that the quality of the performance of our cells and organs drops, leaving them vulnerable to disease. Between the ages of 30 and 90, for example, the reserve capacities of our organs are reduced:

◆ Height reduces by about one-sixteenth of an inch every year from the age of thirty as the space between the vertebrae wear thinner.
◆ Body fat gathers around the thighs and hips.
◆ The speed of nerve responses drops by 15 per cent.
◆ Skin becomes less elastic, taking longer to settle after being pinched.
◆ Most men gradually lose their original 100,000 scalp hairs.
◆ The amount of blood our heart can pump in a minute drops by 30 per cent.
◆ Wounds take longer to heal.
◆ The filtration rate of our kidneys is reduced by 40 per cent.
◆ The largest amount of air we can breathe in and out in a minute is reduced by 60 per cent.
◆ Sleep patterns change: we sleep less and snore more.
◆ Muscles, joints and bones become weaker.
◆ The immune system is less efficient.
◆ Sight, hearing, smell, taste and balance may begin to fail.
◆ Memory and thought processes may become confused.
◆ Body temperature control may lessen.
◆ The menopause brings ovarian functioning to a close and by 70, two-thirds of men have erectile dysfunction.
◆ Food intake is reduced.

None of these changes is inevitable in everyone and their seriousness will vary in each individual. Princess Metternich, when asked at what age a woman ceased to be capable of sexual love, said: 'I do not know, I am only sixty-five.'

To a certain degree, we can foresee our own future by looking at the medical biographies of our parents and grandparents: we are carrying the genes that kept them fit until their late nineties or those that were behind their chronic heart disease.

The older we get, the more genetic complications occur and the more vulnerable we become to accident, infection and other disease: cells becomes less able to repair, energise and detoxify themselves. There are some diseases – heart disorders, strokes, atherosclerosis, auto-immune disorders and cancers – which are particularly identified with old age. This is because there are often a number of causes behind them and it may take many years before all the factors come together to produce disabling signs and symptoms.

Hearts

The heart, at the rate of 100,000 daily beats, pumps more than 14,000 pints of blood around the body each day in order to feed it with oxygen. This is so that the freshly nourished blood cells can circulate to sustain the other organs – particularly the brain.

Following a heart attack – causing a reduced oxygen supply to the brain – one in five people will die before reaching a casualty department – one in ten if they can get there within the 'golden' first hour. In the end, 50–60 per cent of people with heart disease will succumb to the first or a subsequent attack.

The overall death rate has improved dramatically since the arrival of new drugs and improved resuscitation techniques. However, the incidence of heart disease is rising. This means that instead of dying, many more people survive to experience the drawn-out, disabling pain of progressive chronic heart failure – an extended, but often miserable, life.

Even if there is no specific disease, the heart, like the rest of us, gradually loses it strength and the ability of its nerves and cells to repair themselves. The fastest the heart can work reduces by one beat per minute every year: take away your age from 220 and you can work out your probable maximum heart rate – unlikely to be exceeded however much you exercise.

Lungs

Everybody dies of the same thing: not enough oxygen. No matter what disease is involved, ultimately the fatal event is that the brain stem dies from lack of nourishment. The lungs harvest this vital gas and our well-being, therefore, depends on the quality of the raw material and the efficiency of its collection from the atmosphere.

With age, there is a drop in the efficiency of the transfer of oxygen to the blood through the lung tissue and we will need to slow down or breathe more deeply to keep up the same performance that we had in our youth. Things are made worse, of course, if we complicate matters by breathing in polluted air – traffic fumes, asbestos dust, tobacco smoke – which lowers the effectiveness of the lungs.

Kidney inefficiency can affect the salt/water balance in the body and this can cause the lungs to become waterlogged. Warm, wet environments are welcome territories for bacterial growth and this may become the site for pneumonia and other dangers.

Kidneys

Between the ages of 40 and 80, our kidneys will reduce in weight by 20 per cent and, after 40, the blood flow to the kidneys will fall by 10 per cent every decade: the narrow blood vessels thicken and restrict the flow further. Over a normal lifetime over half of the filtering capacity of the kidneys is lost, which means that fewer impurities are removed from the urine and their ability to keep a balance of water and salt in the body is reduced – which can lead to heart problems or dehydration.

Bladders

Young bladder tissue is elastic and can stretch and contract easily. As it ages it loses its flexibility and won't hold so much urine. The operation of the valve mechanism controlling the urine flow may become inefficient, causing incontinence; bacteria can gain entrance causing urinary-tract infection.

Brains

The brain weighs about the same as a bag of sugar. Although it makes up only 2 per cent of body weight, it accounts for 20 per cent of the body's energy requirements: after the age of 50, it loses 2 per cent of its weight every decade. We all know that we lose nerve cells in the brain throughout our life: in old age we may only have 50 per cent of our original capacity of cells controlling movement, vision and other sensory faculties.

It's common to find that ageing brains have shrunk slightly. This, combined with the loss of nerve cells, has created a myth that our mental abilities deteriorate with age. This is untrue. Mental capacity is not to do with the *number* of brain cells so much as the development of interconnections between them. A group of older people will not be as quick as younger people in a timed intelligence test but if the time limit is removed they are more successful.

The nerve cells in the higher intellectual areas of the brain are much less likely to be lost and there is some evidence that *their* activity is increased – which may explain the (correct) reputation of older people for wisdom and shrewdness. These higher centres are, however, vulnerable to Alzheimer's disease. Here the degeneration and loss of nerve cells can play havoc with perception, memory, learning and judgement. As little is known about a cure as there is about its cause. In the United Kingdom 700,000 people suffer from Alzheimer's disease.

The other catastrophe that can afflict the brain is a stroke. This is caused by some interference in the blood supply bringing fresh oxygen: the starving nerve tissue can be harmed or can die. Where the site is and the damage caused will determine the severity and location of the stroke symptoms. Approximately a fifth of people who have strokes in hospital die fairly soon afterwards, a third will become disabled and half make a recovery – but most of these will need subsequent institutional or hospital care for the rest of their lives. Again longevity will be achieved at the expense of some quality of life.

> *Life would be infinitely happier if we could only be born at the age of eighty and gradually approach eighteen.*
>
> Mark Twain (1835–1910)

Reproduction and ageing

> *Green ivy, which catchetch an old Tree, maketh quick work for the fire: and the embracements of a faire woman, hastneth an old man to his grave.*
>
> Richard Taverner, 1546

Testosterone, the male reproductive hormone, has unwanted side effects on the body. It tends to suppress the immune system, reducing its protective efficiency; it speeds up deterioration of the artery walls, causing circulation problems;

it also is involved in the development of prostate cancer. Tests on castrated laboratory animals show them to be healthier and longer-lived than sexually active ones.

Not only animals. John Hamilton, in the United States, produced some research in 1969 disclosing startling results. He had discovered some medical records for 300 long-term male patients in a 'mental retardation hospital'. Many years earlier, as was then customary, these men had been castrated because of their 'behaviour problems'. When he compared this group with 700 contemporaries in the institution he discovered that those who had been castrated lived almost 14 years longer than those who hadn't. The earlier it had been done, the longer they lived.

Women's reproductive hormones may also cause similar life-shortening side effects. So early castration and sterilisation may be a shrewd (if ill-advised) option for adding years on to your life (if not life on to your years).

Life is a sexually transmitted terminal disease with a fatality rate of 100 per cent.

Anon

If only we could cure cancer and heart disease...

The remarkable thing is that if, by some completely impossible advance in medical technology, we were able to successfully treat the major causes of death and no one ever died from cancer, heart attack, diabetes, accident, etc., this miracle would only increase our life-expectancy by about twelve years. And it would not extend our maximum life span beyond its present limits.

Cause of death eliminated	Years gained
Heart disease	6.42
Cancers	2.23
Stroke	0.88
Respiratory disease	0.69
Influenza and pneumonia	0.27
Cirrhosis of liver	0.28
Bronchitis	0.27

Emphysema and asthma	0.27
Diabetes	0.16
Vehicle accidents	0.21
All other accidents	0.28
Total gain by elimination of all common causes of death	11.79

If no one were to die from one of the common killing diseases or accidents, how then would we die? Excluding such things as wars and natural catastrophes, virtually all of us would die from senility, i.e. the slow disintegration caused by biological ageing.

> *In other words, unless ageing is 'cured', then all of the massive amount of intensive care and high-tech medicine for the cure of the major causes of death will yield very little in terms of lengthening individual life-span and probably nothing in terms of bettering the quality of that life. In fact, it seems obvious that, by forcing everyone into senility, this type of medicine will substantially decrease the quality of individual life and erode the social fabric.*
>
> Chadd Everone, PhD 1998,
> The Life-Extension and Control of Ageing Programme

After our middle years, the direction of our health is downwards: we *may* succumb in our fifties but most of us will achieve our sixties to seventies.

The oldest reliably recorded person who has ever lived is Jeanne Calment who lived in Arles in the South of France. She came from a famously long-lived family and she died in 1997 aged 122 years. In spite of it being such a recent record, it is likely that many people in the past – even the distant past – have lived this long if they have survived the dangers of their earlier life and times. However, this is likely to be near the limit for the far foreseeable future.

You will hear tales of extremely long-lived people – 150 years and beyond. There is usually no way of verifying the truth of their claims but we are fascinated to discover their secret. (Maybe the best way to be long lived is to live in a gullible society with very poor records of births and deaths.)

It is, however, *illegal* to die of 'old age'. A death certificate is not accepted unless a specific cause is given.

We tend to think that 'medical science' has had a dramatic effect in prolonging our lives: the truth is much more modest. It has been said that the total medical progress of the last 50 years has increased life expectancy by only five years.

Another misconception is that deaths are always caused by 'big' incurable diseases. However, 33 per cent of all deaths of people over 85 years are caused, not by serious diseases, but by simple infections and traumas which a younger person with a shiny new immune system would easily be able to take in their stride.

> *I've never known a person to live to be one hundred and be remarkable for anything else.*
>
> Henry Wheeler Shaw (1818–1885)

Fear of dying

> *Nor dread nor hope attend*
> *A dying animal*
> *A man awaits his end*
> *Dreading and hoping all.*
>
> W. B. Yeats, 'Death'

Death-fearing folk live longer?

> *Self-decapitation is an extremely difficult, not to say dangerous, thing to attempt.*
>
> W. S. Gilbert (1836–1911)

Fearing death has a great evolutionary advantage. The parent who shouts at their toddler who is sticking a finger in the electric socket: 'What do you think you're doing – you'll be killed!' is sensibly reinforcing the child's genetic impulse to survive.

However, in this way, we have developed a culture that dramatises and stresses possible bad outcomes and the concept of 'death' is painted as something to be feared.

We grow up to see death as being worse than *anything* because it is definitely the one thing which will prevent us completing our genetic destiny. Similarly, murder is viewed as the most terrible of crimes – the worst thing you can do to someone. In many countries we reserve the 'most terrible punishment' for murder – capital punishment.

So the concept of death is usually painted in a negative way.

But what, after all, is there to be frightened of?

> *There was a time when we were not: this gives us no concern.*
> *To die is only to be as we were before we were born.*
> William Hazlitt (17777788226018892) *Fear of Death*

In a television play in June 1998, *Spoonface Sternberg* by Lee Hall, a seven-year-old dyslexic girl who is terminally ill muses about the emptiness of non-existence. The playwright's masterly use of back-to-front language expresses a shining fearlessness:

> *If I wasn't scared of when I wasn't born, why would I be scared of when I wasn't existed at the other end?*
> *... When you think about dying it is very hard to do. It is to think about what is not – to think about everything that there is nothing: to not be and never to be again. It is even more than emptiness. If you think of emptiness it is full of nothing and death is more than this. Death is even less than nothing.*
> *When you think about that you will not be here for your breakfast, that you will not see Mum or Dad... or the tele...or feel anything any more. But you wouldn't feel sad as there would be nothing to feel of. Not that there is even anything. There is not even nothing. And that is death....*
> *Everywhere there'll be something in the whole world. Everything will be full – except me. And there isn't even a hole somewhere where I used to be. And apart from people that remember me, and what I was like, there is nothing missing from when I was here. There is no space in the Universe where people have dropped out. It's all filled in as full as ever....*
> *And every moment is forever; and it will shine and it will be everything and nothing and that is all there is to know; that all of us will end up being one and that is nothing. And it is endless.*

Where there's life...

We grow up to see and admire the efforts of doctors finding ever more ingenuous ways of keeping us from being dead. We wonder over the energy that hospitals and families put into keeping grossly disabled people alive who seem to have no understanding of what is happening around them and seem to be in great distress. Anything is better than death – isn't it?

We can be moved at the hope and commitment involved in situations like this, but we're left with the implication that if such a desolate, unrewarding life is better than death, how much more dreadful death must be.

Although this in-built horror about death hovering around, threatening to thwart our genetic destiny, is stubborn, it can be reduced and as we get older there is evidence that it does subside.

Pipes and slippers

As we go through life, establishing a career and family, we gradually go a long way to achieving our personal and social goals (if we're lucky, or we work at it). The crucial importance of survival takes a lesser place than it did when we were in our teens and on the threshold of making our way in the world.

Death will no longer be a crucial interference with our plans for life.

> *I have a deep sense of change within, and of a permanently closer companionship with death.*
>
> George Eliot on her 50th birthday

We also gain more experience of life and become less self-absorbed than we were in our youth: we see ourselves more in the context of the family and our community – which will continue after we have gone. We 'get ourselves more into proportion' than when we were young and preparing to take on the world single-handed.

> *I know there are many more books in me, but it does not particularly bother me if I write them, or take up painting again, or do the garden. I tiptoe towards age with a husband*

*of 30 years standing, glad that the impulses of wild youth did
not drive him away. With a son of 24 and a daughter of 18
who are a far greater achievement than backpacking across
India ... Music, painting, books and the fields and trees and
wildflowers outside my window matter to me now far more
than they did when I was 30. I am overwhelmed with
richness, and yet I am not afraid of the day when I have to
give them up, and enter the darkness. Or the light.*

Bel Mooney, *The Guardian*, May 1998

Older people have much more information about, and
experience of, death. They will have seen people they know and
love die. Having lived through the ascendancy of youth we have
a greater understanding of the mirror image of our decline.
Open discussion about death is more frequent as we grow older
and we begin to review our lives.

But, then, it's neither death nor dying that we really fear

It's common for people to maintain that it isn't death itself
that they fear but the *process of dying*. Death is a neutral –
perhaps even welcome – consequence of 'dying'.

On the other hand, curiously, we could probably agree with
the philosopher Thomas Nagel who said:

*I would not really object to dying if it were not followed by
death.*

This seems reasonable: most of us could put up with some
days or weeks of frailty, incapacity, even some pain, if we knew
we would make a full recovery.

Many of us could thus find a reason for fearing *neither*
death *nor* the process of dying. So what is 'fear of death' about?

The apparent puzzle is because our fears and anxieties have
little to do with the nothingness of death or the fading away of
dying. What we are afraid of is the *ending of living*.

A consequence of achieving our aims in life is that we grow
attached to our increasing success, standard of living and
personal status. As we see old age and death approach, our
attachment to these begins to be threatened. Our valued sense

of ourselves becomes vulnerable:

◆ Our **capability** might be drastically affected by degenerative changes in the brain.

◆ Our **independence** might be challenged by disability or chronic disease in old age.

◆ Our **family life** will change as our children move away and, perhaps, we face the death of our partner.

◆ Our **standard of living** might be threatened by reduced income and the possibility of greater health and social care charges.

◆ Our **role as a parent** might be reversed with our children – should they need to care for us and we become dependent on them.

◆ Our **bequests of property and money** to our family might be eaten up by long-term residential care charges.

These possibilities become more likely the closer we get to the end of life. So we are fearful.

The more importance we attach to these aspects of personal success and self-esteem, the more keenly the threat of their loss will be (and the greater our fear will be). The less importance we attach to our capabilities, independence, role in life and material possessions, the less we have to lose: the less will be our fear.

> *The fear of dying is the fear of losing what I possess – my body, my ego, my possessions and my identity – to the extent that we live in the 'having' mode, we must fear dying. Losing our fear of dying should not begin as a preparation for death, but as the continuous effort to reduce the mode of having and to increase the mode of being.*
>
> Eric Fromm, *To Have Or To Be,* 1979

In one study about fear of death in those with terminal illnesses, two out of every three under 50 years of age showed extreme anxiety: over the age of 50 the proportion was one in three.

Don't be half-hearted about your religious beliefs

> *The worst part of Christianity is the terror it inculcates upon a deathbed. The wisest dread it; no person who is strictly brought up in the principles of Christianity can ever thoroughly shake off the fear of dying.*
>
> Lady Elizabeth Holland, *Journal*, 1908

Without thinking about it too much, we might guess that people who professed a faith in a life after death would be more settled with the thought of their mortal life ending: this isn't so.

Surveys have found that only one out of five people with firm religious beliefs and one out of four of those with no faith at all were *very anxious* about their impending deaths. Interestingly, three out of five of those people who professed a faith but were not committed practitioners showed great fear of death.

We have less to fear for our future after death if we believe an afterlife is either *definite* or *impossible*: uncertainty about it makes it a fearful unknowable possibility and this might be made worse by guilt feelings about our lack of faith and shortcomings in our conduct in life.

But what about the pain?

This is what most people will reply if you ask them if they fear death. This reflects an outdated assumption that dying is usually associated with pain. It used to be – in the days when our parents were passing on to us their death-attitudes.

> *I am afraid to think about my death;*
> *When it shall be, and whether in great pain*
> *I shall rise up and fight the air for breath,*
> *Or calmly wait the bursting of my brain.*
>
> James Elroy Flecker

In a survey of patients with cancer, only one person in eight suffered 'considerable pain' during their terminal illness. The rest reported a variety of degrees of pain – half were almost pain free.

In almost all cases, pain can be almost fully relieved given good assessment and careful prescription. However, pain is difficult to understand – one person's 'pain' is another's 'irritation'. Professor Leo Strunin, President of the Royal College of Anaesthetists, was reported in the *Independent on Sunday* (20 September 1998):

> *Most pain is treatable and there is no reason why anybody should die in agony... that is simply not acceptable....It seems to be ingrained in the medical-nursing establishment that opoids are bad for you because they'll turn you into an addict. If you're dying of cancer, so what? What you need is a drug to get rid of the pain, maybe very large amounts, but not all my colleagues are comfortable about administering them.*

There are other conditions, which can make life unpleasant for 40 per cent of people who are dying: coughing, difficulty swallowing and breathing, insomnia, dry mouth, fatigue, confusion, loss of appetite, loss of concentration or depression. These problems can be effectively controlled in 60 per cent of patients.

◆ 'Weakness', caused by chemical changes affecting muscle functioning, is suffered by 80 per cent of people.
◆ Nausea and vomiting is suffered by 33 per cent.
◆ Breathlessness affects 40 per cent of people with advanced cancer (70 per cent of lung cancer patients).
◆ Lack of appetite is common (60 per cent) – and natural; nourishment becomes less of a priority. (Some Muslim people may choose to fast as death approaches.)
◆ Constipation (40 per cent) (sometimes caused by painkillers) is common, as is water retention: both can be effectively treated.

When you rate 32 symptoms of distress in dying people, the most prevalent is usually *'fatigue'* and you will normally find *'worrying'*, *'feeling sad'* and *'feeling nervous'* in the top five. Other common symptoms are *'shortness of breath'*, *'confusion'* and *'muscle wasting'*.

Mostly people rate *highly* those symptoms of distress which are associated with some disability or the quality of their life.

There is a relationship between the severity of distress and survival time.

Pain relief and palliative care

However, in recent years a new medical specialism has developed, concerned solely with pain relief, and nowadays most large hospitals have a pain clinic. The pressure for this has undoubtedly come from the hospice movement where pain management has become increasingly sophisticated. St Christopher's – one of the first hospices – claims that pain can be kept under control 98 per cent of the time, without the patient being drugged into semi-unconsciousness.

Another specialism that has emerged during the last few years is 'palliative care'. This is unique in medical care because it has nothing to do with the 'curing' of disease. The overall aim is not to prolong life but to make things as comfortable as possible as death approaches. Again, palliative care has developed from the hospice movement.

There needs to be a single person co-ordinating care – sometimes provided by several others. These teams can be led by specialist district nurses, hospice workers or family doctors. Macmillan nurses and Marie Curie Nurses often have key roles.

It is recognised that pain is a very personal experience: one person may need 100 times the amount of a painkiller as someone else for the same relief to be achieved. Some research in the Department of Pharmaceutical Science at the University of Alberta in 1999 showed that the level of painkiller in the blood of someone suffering searing pain – in this case, wisdom tooth extraction – is much less than in someone who is pain-free and the active ingredients take much longer to have an effect. The body under severe stress stops functioning normally and fails to digest the tablets as quickly or completely. The implications of this are that when someone is in extreme pain, unknown but very large quantities of analgesic may need to be given – an art rather than a science.

People often worry about the use of morphine, heroin and other opiates in pain relief – sometimes 1–2 grams a day. There are public associations with addiction and danger. However, the risks are different in a young, healthy person: these opiates are not psychologically addictive and do not shorten life. The dilemma is that such drugs, whilst removing pain, can cause drowsiness, nausea, dry mouth, sweating, palpitations and mood changes. The trick is to achieve a balance between severe pain and other discomforts.

Often the secret is for the patient to be in charge of her own pain relief. A syringe-driver, or syringe pump, is a small device which she can operate herself. The pump feeds a needle just below the skin through a plastic tube, which delivers a regular supply of analgesic. If necessary the patient can adjust the supply as she wishes.

Patients and their families should not suffer in silence: we have the right to expect avoidable pain and suffering to be removed so that we can give our attention to the more important business of settling and closing relationships.

The older, the easier

Older people suffer less cumulative pain than young people who are more healthy and able to fight harder and longer. Often, other diseases are present and patients may succumb quite quickly without much retaliation.

Over 70 years:	10 per cent of terminally ill people have considerable pain.
Between 50 and 70:	32 per cent of terminally ill people have considerable pain.
Under 50 years:	45 per cent of terminally ill people have considerable pain.

But remember: if you seek out the right treatment, 98 per cent of this pain can be controlled. It's also worth noting that there is a wide variation in how different people tolerate the same degree of pain so what might be 'considerable' for me might, after a paracetamol, be negligible for you.

We must also bear in mind, to keep things in proportion, that not only are the large majority of terminally ill patients free of unbearable pain, but one person in four dies completely pain-free, peacefully and in a state of acceptance and resignation.

More people used to be born – and died young

> *Of all the children that are born, scarcely one half reach*
> *adolescence, and it is very likely that your pupil will not live*
> *to be a man.*
>
> Rousseau, *Emile* (about education in the eighteenth century)

> *'How many brothers and sisters have you, little girl?'*
> *'We are seven, sir. Three at home and three in the graveyard.'*
>
> Mid-nineteenth-century conversation

In the past, people had many children with the expectation that
many would be lost because of miscarriage or stillbirth or
would die in infancy: in the 1840s in Manchester, 40 per cent
of all children died before the age of five. Death was an
everyday occurrence.

One-third of all the money deposited in savings banks in
the middle of the nineteenth century was saved in order to pay
funeral expenses.

> *One woman who was keeping a child from charity, a fine boy*
> *of nine, said she would like to send him to school but could*
> *not afford the 2d a week as she paid 1d for a burial club for*
> *him, poor fellow.*
>
> Nancy Mitford, *The Ladies of Alderley*

Nowadays, because of a dramatic reduction in the infant
mortality rate and because women's lives have expanded
beyond simple motherhood, families are able to plan to have
fewer children with almost assured health. It is very unusual to
hear of the death of a child – in this country, at least:

> *Question 1. Do you have any children?*
> *Question 2. Are any of them still alive?*
>
> Nigel Barley, *Dancing on the Grave* (quoting an African tax form)

In 1840 in Britain, 148 babies were stillborn for every 1,000
live births. In the 1980s the rate was 8 per 1,000. Death,
therefore, is much less present and evident within the normal
family setting. The increased value we place on youth and

health tends to distance us from age, disease and death. The national shock at Princess Diana's death was, partially, a reflection of the rarity of young death: 100 years ago, of all those born on the same day as her, more than half would already have predeceased her.

When a death happens to someone we know, it is unusual and its impact tends to be strong. In 1710 it was acceptable for an American diarist to record, as though it was something that happened every day:

> *After the funeral my wife continued to be exceedingly afflicted for the loss of her child; notwithstanding, I comforted her as well as I could. I ate calf's head for dinner.*
>
> William Byrd, about the death of his two-year-old son

The place where we die has changed

> *No pleasure is worth giving up for the sake of two more years in a geriatric home at Weston-Super-Mare.*
>
> Kingsley Amis

Nowadays we have very little familiarity with death – it mostly happens unseen, away from home. Because we are not used to death, we lack the necessary knowledge, skills and experience to discuss it. How often do we see a dramatic scene portraying a natural death on television?

There is an unconscious legacy – even for atheists – of the long-standing connection between heaven, hell, purgatory and death. We approach a mysterious, vaguely supernatural area of life. We prefer to talk about illness, with the implication of a possible cure, rather than admit someone is dying. Death is failure.

A century ago the overwhelming majority of people died at home. Family members lived closer and it was accepted that they would look after each other. It was understood that people died of 'old age' and they expected to be and were used to being around when relatives and neighbours died. Friends and relatives would see it as a sign of respect to see, touch or kiss the dead person. In the 1950s twice as many people died at home as do now.

Death was not a medical occasion: it was a family and social affair. There was neither the medical capability nor eagerness to pursue complex treatments requiring hospital care. Now our expectations of medical care have increased and most of us expect access to the very latest treatment, irrespective of resources. We are much more aware of what could be available and not to provide it seems like negligence.

We also live alone more than we ever have – especially older people. Forty per cent of women between 65 and 74 years live on their own (it's 61 per cent for those over 75).

Dying in hospital

When we become frail, if there is no family or other adequate help, hospital becomes inevitable. Most people, therefore, spend their last days in hospitals or nursing homes. One-third of people who die in hospital do so within a few hours of admission. Of the majority who survive, there is no doubt that their lives are longer for it. However:

◆ Going into hospital removes the experience of death from the community and hides it away.
◆ It changes it from a natural life event – taking place in the family – to a medical failure.
◆ It reduces family and social contacts during the final illness. Three-quarters of people in hospital who lived with partners when they were at home die with no one present. Only 15 per cent of those at home die alone.
◆ The hospital environment is also hostile to the needs of dying people and their families: they are busy, public places with little opportunity for privacy.

Medical care is focused on improving life rather than making death more comfortable. It is not uncommon for someone's last days to be dominated by discussion of 'further tests' or 'changing the medication'. Many people's last awareness of life includes thumps on the chest or electric shocks to the heart. The temptation to resuscitate 'at all costs' is high.

There is a low emphasis on terminal care in medical and nursing training: one survey found 50 per cent of junior doctors unhappy about the lack of suitable training.

'Where there's life, there's hope' – even if there isn't.

Dying in residential care

In the absence of clear medical indications, many older people live in residential care homes if they can no longer remain unsupported at home. In spite of recent improvements, these often remain 'institutions' with little to offer that a family home can provide. They are often 'peaceful', subdued places where a lonely death can take place quietly: there is often little opportunity or encouragement for staff or other residents to show any signs of bereavement.

It is estimated that one in five of us will eventually need full-time residential care, where people die, on average, two years after admission. It's not uncommon for the shock of the change of environment to result in death within weeks. On average, between a quarter and a third of residents in a home will die in any one year.

Within the social work profession there is an emphasis on quality of life for residents but less attention to quality of dying. Staff are poorly trained and often kept too busy to sit with a dying person. So often a death is met with embarrassment and secrecy: a dying resident might be kept away from the other residents and will 'disappear' the moment they die. There is often little discussion encouraged amongst the staff and other residents. There is risk that the needs of the 'institution' will predominate.

In August 1998 it was reported that Castle Morpeth District Council in Northumberland was in dispute with a local private residential home over the payment of funeral expenses for one of the residents. Local authorities have an obligation to pay under the 1984 Public Health Act where no other source can be identified. Because her savings had run out and there were no relatives, the home applied for funding. In reply, declining the request, the council argued:

from a commercial viewpoint, residents of a home are its income-producing raw material. Ergo, from a purely commercial view, deceased residents may then be regarded as being the waste produced by their business.

Such thoughtlessness is untypical but it gives an idea of the sort of depersonalisation that can creep into institutional care.

Death language

He entered into rest, suddenly, and, mercifully, pegged out.

In *Roget's Thesaurus* there are 17 column centimetres giving alternative words for 'life': there are 90 column centimetres setting out the verbal contortions we have invented to explain mortality away.

If you look at headstones in cemeteries from before the middle of the nineteenth century you will find plain and simple language:

Here lies the body of...
Beneath this stone are the mortal remains...

During the late Victorian times, however, the language began to change. We may think of the Victorians as being much more comfortable about the subject of death than us, but that doesn't mean that their interest was simple and healthy. Death was less accepted as a physical fact and seen more as a sentimental, gentle transition into some fanciful, mock spiritual state. The euphemisms that persist today began to creep in. Death was described in terms of welcome rest: 'falling asleep', 'at peace'.

By the 1920s these softening phrases had almost taken over from direct language. They have reflected the growing difficulty we have had in facing up to the reality of death. There was also a growing concept, as we developed a strong sense of our own individuality, that life has been hard, grinding and burdensome: death comes to be seen as a welcome respite – 'we deserve a rest'.

These metaphors are comforting and harmless enough if they protect our sensibilities, but they paint false pictures for young children. These may linger with them for life and help set in the confusion we have all had in our attitude to the subject. Telling a child that her mother has 'gone to sleep' or 'gone away' is intended as a kindness, but it is dishonest as well as potentially harmful: what is she to think when her older brother 'goes away' to university? When she 'goes to sleep' at night will she ever wake up?

Whilst we can all understand that we should learn to be direct in the way that we speak about death, it is very difficult to achieve. We have mostly been brought up within a conspiracy of silence on the whole subject. Imagine beginning a conversation with the following questions:

> *'When do you think you are going to die?'*
> *'How will you go about arranging my funeral?'*
> *'Can I show you my plan for your funeral to see if you approve?'*
> *'Have you considered donating your body for dissection?'*
> *'Do you think these clothes would be suitable for me to be buried in?'*
> *'I don't want anyone to lay out my body: do you know what to do?'*
> *'Could we use your van to take my body to the crematorium?'*

Difficult? It's hard to write them down and difficult to imagine putting such thoughts into words. It's challenging even to speak such questions aloud with no one else in the room, such is the taboo against directness. We also have a feeling that to put concrete words to such thoughts releases some magic power to bring forward the actual fact of death.

The difficulty we have with the language of death can be overcome. I remember the days when it was difficult, in exactly the same way, to talk easily about sexuality. Because of some unspoken social agreement we have mostly been able to throw off this inhibition and talk comfortably about orgasms and erections. Will it ever be possible to talk as easily about shrouds and body bags as we can about condoms and spermicides?

CHAPTER 2

When Will You Die?

Millions long for immortality who don't know what to do with themselves on a rainy Sunday afternoon.
SUSAN ERTZ

*Y*ou are not discontented, surely, because you weigh only so many pounds and not three hundred? So, too, because you may only live so many years and no longer? As you are contented with the quantity of matter determined for you, so also be contented with the length of your days.

The Meditations of Marcus Aurelius, AD 121–180

In the nineteenth century, life expectancy was 41 years: now most people who die are elderly – 80 per cent of all deaths are of people over 80 years old.

◆ Sixty per cent of people over 65 years are women.
◆ Over 85 years, there are 250 women alive for every 100 men.
◆ There are 4 women aged 100 years for every 1 man.
◆ In the 1980s, 75 per cent of all deaths were people over the age of 65.
◆ In the 1920s, 34 per cent of all deaths were people over the age of 65.

By the year 2050 the number of people over 75 will have doubled; the number of people over 90 will have tripled. One in every two girls born in the year 2000 should live to see 2100.

The number of centenarians in the UK has increased dramatically:

1951 – 271
1971 – 1,185
1991 – 4,400
2030 – 30,000 (expected)

In the next couple of years the average English age will be over 40 years for the first time.

The percentage of European people over the age of 60 in the year 2000 will be 21.6. In 1960 it was 15.5 per cent.

What about you?

> *The rather innocent Dr. Fioriuchi thought for a few minutes and then replied quite uncomfortably, 'One year and a half; perhaps two years if you take good care of yourself.'*
>
> *I told Fioriuchi that I had expected to live only five or six months and that in one year I could certainly reap a rich harvest from life. Some of you may say that one year and a half is very short; I say it is an eternity. But if you wish to say it is short, then ten years is also short, and fifty years is short, and so, too, is one hundred years.*
>
> Nakae Chomin, *One Year and a Half*

It's possible, using the Life Tables of the UK Government Actuary's Department – and adjusting them by adding or subtracting various lifestyle and genetic factors – to determine, roughly, what our personal life expectancy might be. These are, of course, averages and do not take into account changes we have made, or might make in the future, to alter our chances of living a longer (or shorter) life. Each year these figures increase by a couple of months with younger men making a slightly greater increase than women – although the differential remains.

Look down the following columns and find your present age. Look across to the 'male' or 'female' column and work out your estimated basic life expectancy in years (you might have to guess at an 'in between' figure).

Average life expectancy

Age now	Men	Women
0 years	74.1 yrs	79.4 yrs
5 years	69.7 yrs	74.9 yrs
10 years	64.8 yrs	69.9 yrs
15 years	59.8 yrs	64.5 yrs
20 years	55.0 yrs	60.1 yrs
25 years	50.3 yrs	55.1 yrs

30 years	45.5 yrs	50.2 yrs
35 years	40.7 yrs	45.4 yrs
40 years	36.0 yrs	40.5 yrs
45 years	31.3 yrs	35.8 yrs
50 years	26.8 yrs	31.2 yrs
55 years	22.4 yrs	26.7 yrs
60 years	18.4 yrs	22.4 yrs
65 years	14.7 yrs	18.6 yrs
70 years	11.5 yrs	14.6 yrs
75 years	8.8 yrs	11.3 yrs
80 years	6.6 yrs	8.5 yrs
85 years	4.9 yrs	6.2 yrs

Government Actuary's Department, 1999

Now continue by adding or subtracting years to match your personal situation. You can do this by responding (honestly) to these searching questions.

The genetic and lifestyle variables

1. If your father lived to be over 70, add one year.
2. If your father lived to be over 80, add two years.
3. If your father lived to be over 85, add three years.
4. If your mother lived to be over 70, add one year.
5. If your mother lived to be over 80, add two years.
6. Have you a grandparent or parent who died of a heart attack, stroke or arteriosclerosis before the age of 50? Subtract two years for each one.
7. For any who died from a heart attack or stroke between the ages of 51 and 60, subtract one year for each one.
8. Have any of your family predecessors had diabetes, thyroid disorders or cancer (and you're not taking any special precautions as advised by your doctor)? If so, subtract one year for each disorder.
9. If you live in an average industrialised society, make no change.
10. If you live in an advanced technological society, add two years.
11. If you live in an emerging industrial society, subtract five years.

12. If you live in the south-east or the west of England, add three years.
13. If you live in Greater London add one year.
14. If you live in the north or east of England, subtract one year.
15. If you live in Scotland, subtract three years.
16. If you live in a small town add four years.
17. If you live in a city, subtract two years.
18. If you graduated from university, add one year.
19. If you have been poor, or wealthy, for most of your life, deduct three years.
20. If you have a professional job, add two years.
21. If you are a civil servant, clerk or secretary, add one year.
22. If you have a skilled job, add nothing.
23. If you have a skilled job involving a lot of exercise, add two years.
24. If you have a partly skilled job, subtract two years.
25. If you have an unskilled job, subtract five years.
26. If you are married and under 30 years, add five years.
27. If you are married and over 30 years but less than 60, add two years.
28. If you are married and over 60 years, add nothing.
29. If you are a separated man living alone, take off nine years; seven if you are a widower living alone. If you are a separated man living with others, take off only half these figures.
30. Women who are separated, take off four years; widows, three and a half – two, if living with others.
31. Women who cannot have children, or plan none, subtract half a year. Women with over seven children, deduct one year.
32. Add a year if you have one or two close friends in whom you can confide.
33. How do friends or relations describe you?
    always calm – add five years
    usually calm – add three years
    moderately calm – add one year
    usually tense – subtract three years
    always tense – subtract five years
34. If you are first-born, add one year.
35. Add two years if your intelligence is above average.
36. If you regularly enjoy 'mind-stretching' activities, add two years.

37. If you have had more than one breakdown, subtract six years.
38. If in recent years your weight has not varied by more than 5lb above or below your ideal weight, add five years.
39. If you are more than a stone underweight, subtract one year.
40. If you are over 30 years and up to half a stone overweight, subtract two years.
41. If you are over 30 years and up to a stone overweight, subtract three years.
42. If you are over 30 years and up to two stones overweight, subtract five years.
43. If you are over 30 years and *more* than two stones overweight, subtract six years.
44. If you miss meals frequently, if you do not regularly eat two or three meals per day (including breakfast), and if you eat hurriedly, subtract one year.
45. Subtract one year for *each* of the following types of food which you eat regularly:
    – fast food
    – refined sugar
    – fatty foods
    – salty foods
46. If you eat at least one meal a day containing food from the basic food groups (meat, dairy products, grains, pulses, vegetables), add two years.
47. If you regularly eat a range of raw vegetables and fruit or take a multivitamin and mineral daily or extra vitamin A, C or E, add one year. If you eat a high fibre food daily, add one year.
48. If you are a *small* drinker of alcohol (i.e. one glass of wine, one measure of spirits or half a pint of beer per day), add one year.
49. If you have more than two drinks of alcohol per day, subtract two years.
50. For every two drinks after that, subtract two years.
51. If you drink half a bottle of spirits or its equivalent a day, subtract ten years.
52. If you drink more, subtract 15 years.
53. If you smoke a pipe or cigars occasionally, subtract two years.
54. If you smoke a pipe or cigars regularly, subtract three years.
55. If you smoke more than 40 cigarettes per day, subtract ten

years.

56. If you smoke more than 20 cigarettes per day, subtract six years.

57. If you smoke 10–20 cigarettes per day, subtract three years.

58. If you do not smoke but live or work with smokers, subtract two years.

59. If you exercise for half an hour or more at least three times a week, add two years. (N.B. Only the more strenuous, aerobically sustained exercising counts – such as swimming, cycling, jogging, etc.)

60. If you walk or run six miles a day (or its equivalent), add five years.

61. If you never exercise, subtract five years.

62. If you regularly sleep fewer than five hours a day or more than nine hours, subtract two years.

63. If you lead a mentally active life, add one year.

64. If you are often bored or depressed, subtract one year.

65. If you are basically happy, add one year.

66. If you have regular sex – once or twice a week – add two years.

67. If you are under chronic emotional stress or anxiety, subtract two years.

68. If you are highly aggressive, competitive or easily irritated, subtract one year.

69. If you live in a polluted environment, subtract one year.

70. If you work in a polluted environment, subtract three years.

71 If you frequently take drugs for recreational purposes, subtract two years.

72. If you're frequently ill, take off five years.

73. If you are often ill, subtract two years.

74. If you never visit a doctor, subtract one year.

75. If you visit your doctor only for regular check-ups, add two years.

76. If you are under 40 and have false teeth, subtract two years.

77. If you are over 50 years and have your own teeth, add two years.

Adapted from: *Manual of Principles and Practices*, The Foundation for Infinite Survival 1995.

In the back of our minds we have the figure of 70 as the

expected human life span. What we don't always realise is that this is the expectation of life of a newborn baby: the longer we live, the more risks we have avoided and the greater becomes our expected life span.

What is discouraging about the above adjustments is the dramatic effect our genetics, environment and lifestyle can have on our death dates. Someone with a near maximum number of years to subtract should anticipate a statistically early death on their thirtieth birthday. What is exciting is how we can alter many of these factors to win some extra years. I feel better already.

(Some of you, I know, will unfortunately have discovered in the above calculations that you died some years ago.)

Now, recalculate your life expectancy – this time answering the questions honestly.

What will be the cause of your death?

Figure 1 shows how various causes of death are distributed amongst various age groups, first for men and secondly for women. The figures relate to the United Kingdom as a whole for the year 1996. They're expressed as a percentage of the

Men	Age 0–1	Age 1–14	Age 15–24	Age 25–34	Age 35–54	Age 55–64	Age 65–74	Age 75+
Circulatory diseases	4	5	4	9	33	43	45	45
Cancer	1	16	7	10	28	37	33	22
Respiratory diseases	10	7	4	5	5	7	12	20
Injury & poisoning	4	30	63	51	15	3	1	1
Infectious diseases	7	8	2	5	3	1	–	–
Other causes	74	34	20	20	16	9	9	12
Total numbers	2600	1100	2800	4700	22600	35100	81700	155900
						Total male deaths		306500

Women	Age 0–1	Age 1–14	Age 15–24	Age 25–34	Age 35–54	Age 55–64	Age 65–74	Age 75+
Circulatory diseases	6	6	7	12	18	29	39	47
Cancer	1	18	17	26	52	48	36	15
Respiratory diseases	9	7	5	6	5	9	13	19
Injury & poisoning	6	23	43	28	8	2	1	1
Infectious diseases	6	8	4	5	1	1	1	–
Other causes	72	38	24	23	16	11	10	18
Total numbers	1900	800	1100	2200	14500	21500	58200	232000
						Total female deaths		332400

Fig. 1. Causes of death, UK, 1996.
Source: General Register Office for Scotland; Northern Ireland Statistics and Research Agency.

other causes for that age group.

Until recently the only way that we could find out the outcome of our lives was with the dubious help of a clairvoyant or palmist. As we enter the new millennium, however, we are on the verge of an awesome period when we will have the possibility of learning much more accurate information about our own life expectancy.

Genetic research is revealing more and more about our individual genetic make-up: tests are being rapidly developed which can give an accurate prognosis for our medical futures. Already there are reliable tests that can predict:

◆ diabetes
◆ Alzheimer's disease
◆ Huntington's chorea
◆ breast cancer
◆ cardiovascular disease
◆ thrombosis
◆ salt-sensitive hypertension
◆ melanoma predisposition.

Source: *The Observer*, December 1998

The problem is that although good predictions can be made, the whole story is not available – in particular, it is not always clear how other factors, such as pollution or nutrition, might influence outcomes.

In addition, as more and more diseases become predictable, what should we do?

◆ Should testing be available through the NHS? Extending it from a 'diagnose and treat' to a 'predict and prevent' service? This would carry massive resource implications.
◆ What happens then? There is not necessarily any treatment available.
◆ If the NHS doesn't provide a testing service, will commercial, unregulated agencies move into the business?
◆ Shall we end up with a large group of 'worried well' people or anxious 'dead men walking'?
◆ What happens to the concepts of pensions and life insurance?

These are all questions with which our children will have to grapple as the twenty-first century unfolds: our attitudes to mortality are going, forcibly, to be challenged.

It's worse for men

For every 100 girl babies, 125 boys are conceived. By the time they are born, however, the ratio will have changed (in the United Kingdom) to 100:106. Boys are not very good at surviving until birth.

And not much good afterwards. In their first year 54 boys will die for every 46 girls. By the age of 21 years, 68 men will die for every 32 women. Men will always die at a higher rate than women of the same age until their 75th year when the proportions will be reversed because the statistics will have nearly run out of living men.

Women tend to die less often than men from the same disease: about the same number of men and women suffer from asthma, but the death rate in men is 30 per cent higher.

> *Females suffering from the same infectious diseases as males die at a much lower rate. A comparison of groups of males and females who smoked equally large numbers of cigarettes showed that females generally were more resistant than males to such deleterious effects as lung cancer and heart disease. Females obviously possess some superior capacity for survival that has little to do with the kinds of lives they lead.*
>
> Peter Farb, *Humankind*, Cape 1978

Because of their greater expectancy of life, women have much more experience of death. Their lives seem to be filled with carefully spaced 'practice' losses – of virginity, independence (less true these days), career after childbirth, childcare roles as children go to school and later leave home, and ovulation and childbearing capacity. They are more likely to see their male partners and friends die and will have more time left to consider their own mortality.

In addition, throughout their lives, women (for all sorts of reasons) have been traditionally more involved than men with family relationships and physical and emotional care: they have been much more used to becoming engaged in situations involving loss and bereavement. This is changing as gender expectations become more equal.

Although in the past women were socially disadvantaged as widows because they were considered 'appendages' of their partners, this will not be true of future generations. Similarly, the helplessness of a new widower, who had never cooked a meal or been shopping, will soon be a thing of the past.

Our chances of surviving cancer are greater if we are women. In a massive study (three million patients) over 25 years, a recent study showed that a higher percentage of women consistently survived a range of cancers for at least one year:

	Men	Women
Oesophagus	21 per cent	25 per cent
Stomach	23 per cent	26 per cent
Rectum	65 per cent	66 per cent
Pancreas	9 per cent	10 per cent
Lung	19 per cent	19 per cent
Bone	69 per cent	71 per cent
Skin melanoma	90 per cent	94 per cent
Brain	28 per cent	30 per cent

More women also survive bowel, head and neck cancers, leukaemias and non-Hodgkins lymphoma. In the longer term the differences are even more dramatic – 82 per cent of women suffering from skin cancer survived longer than five years compared with 68 per cent of men.

This is partly due to the fact that the commonest cancers in women have naturally higher survival rates, but, more importantly, women are much more sensitive to their health and are more prepared to go to their GP with early symptoms.

> *Curious fact.* In 1990, according to the US National Weather Bureau, 67 men died from lightning strikes, but only 7 women – there's probably a very reasonable explanation....

How long would you *like* to live?

One of our implied aims in life is to live as long as possible.
But what does that actually mean?

> *Those who wish to abolish death (whether by physical or*
> *metaphysical means) – at what stage of life do they want the*
> *process to be halted? At the age of twenty? At thirty-five, in*
> *our prime? To be thirty-five for two years sounds attractive,*
> *certainly. But for three years? A little dull, surely. For five years*
> *– ridiculous. For ten – tragic.*
>
> *The film is so absorbing that we want this bit to go on and*
> *on. You mean, you want the projector stopped, to watch a*
> *single motionless frame? No, no, no, but. . .*
>
> *Perhaps you'd like the whole sequence made up as an*
> *endless band, and projected indefinitely? Not that, either.*
>
> *The sea and the stars and the wastes of the desert go on*
> *forever, and will not die. But the sea and the stars and the*
> *wastes of the desert are dead already.*
>
> Michael Frayn, *Constructions*

It's an intriguing question.

Considering what we know about the inevitability of the
ageing process, can we name the age when we would like our
life to end?

We all know about Gulliver's adventures in Lilliput.
However, he made a lesser known stop-off in the land of the
Struldbruggs:

> *When they came to four score years, which is reckoned the*
> *extremity of living in this country, they had not only all the*
> *follies and infirmities of other old men, but many more which*
> *arose from the dreadful prospect of never dying.*
>
> *They were not only opinionative, peevish, covetous, morose,*
> *vain, talkative; but uncapable of friendship and dead to all*
> *natural affection, which never descended below their*
> *grandchildren.*
>
> *Envy and impotent desires, are their prevailing passions.*
> *But those objects against which their envy seems principally*
> *directed, are the vices of the younger sort, and the deaths of the*

*old. By reflecting on the former, they find themselves cut off
from all possibility of pleasure; and whenever they see a
funeral, they lament and repine that others are gone to a
harbour of rest, to which they themselves never can hope to
arrive.*

*They have no remembrance of any thing but what they
learned and observed in their youth and middle age, and even
that is very imperfect. . . .*

*The least miserable among them, appear to be those who
turn to dotage, and entirely lose their memories;, these meet
with more pity and assistance, because they want many bad
qualities, which abound in others.*

Jonathan Swift, *Gulliver's Travels*

There are ways of living for ever

As to posterity, I may ask what it has ever done for us.

Thomas Gray (1716–1771)

There are different sorts of immortality:

Biological

Living through our descendants:

*Life is a flame that is always burning itself out: but it catches
fire again every time a child is born.*

George Bernard Shaw

We do, literally, continue to have a physical presence in the
world long after our deaths. Just as we have carried forward a
part of our ancestors' genetic material, so we, jointly with our
partners, have passed on actual physical DNA material to our
own children.

*Much later that night, my daughter came down to the kitchen
in her nightie. 'Dad will never see the man I marry.' I nodded.
'No, he won't. He always hoped he'd live to see you have your
babies, but he won't now. But when you have your own
children, one day Dad will look up at you from your child's*

face. Just occasionally, my father smiles up at me from yours.'
Mary Jones, *Secret Flowers*, The Women's Press 1988

However, there are less tangible legacies we give to future
generations: our attitudes to life, our way of living,
communicating and relating to other people. We have inherited
these from our parents and we will, together with our spouse,
adapt them further. By combining our DNA and our lifestyle
examples, we (our partners and ourselves) can hope that our
children will benefit from the best of these attributes.

Creative

The continuing influence we may have on others and the world
after we are gone. The poet Robert Frost has a poem – 'Never
Again Will Birds' Song Be The Same' – in which a father
reflects on how his young dead daughter's happiness lived on
in nature. It ends:

Admittedly an eloquence so soft
Could only have an influence on birds
When call or laughter carried it aloft.
Be that as it may, she was in their song.
Moreover, her voice, upon their voices crossed,
Had now persisted in the woods so long
That probably it never would be lost.
Never again would birds' song be the same
And to do that to birds was why she came.

Robert Frost

Natural

Ashes to ashes, dust to dust:

The death of each of us is in the order of things. It follows life
as surely as night follows day. We can take the Tree of Life as
a symbol. The human race is the trunk and branches of the
tree and the individual men and women are the leaves, which
appear one season, flourish for a summer, and then die. I, too,
am like a leaf of this tree, and one day I shall be torn off by a

storm, or simply decay and fall – and become part of the earth about its roots.

But while I live, I am conscious of the tree's flowing sap and steadfast strength. Deep down in my consciousness is a consciousness of a collective life of which I am a part, and to which I make a minute but unique contribution. When I die and fall the tree remains, nourished to some small degree by my manifestation of life. Millions of leaves have preceded me and millions will follow me, but the tree itself grows and endures.

The Meditations of Marcus Aurelius, AD 121–80

Experiential

The way in which transcendental experiences put day-to-day life in perspective:

I do not know what I seem to the world, but to myself I appear to have been like a boy playing on the seashore and diverting myself by now and then finding a smoother pebble or prettier shell than ordinary, while the great ocean of truth lay before me all undiscovered.

Sir Isaac Newton on his deathbed, 1727

By moving ourselves away from centre stage, we become aware of the vastness of creation and the universe: our personal part in the scheme of things becomes insignificant and our births and deaths become as important as the life cycle of a butterfly or an ant.

An individual human existence should be like a river – small at first, narrowly contained within its banks and rushing passionately past boulders and over waterfalls.

Gradually the river grows wider, the banks recede, the waters flow more gently and in the end, without any visible break, they become merged in the sea, and painlessly lose their individual being.

The man or woman who, in old age, can see their life in this way will not suffer from fear of death, since the things they care for will continue.

Bertrand Russell

Theological

Half the British population believe in immortality in the religious sense, a quarter have no belief and a quarter are not sure. The majority of people in the world have beliefs that include some form of continuity beyond this life.

> *Oh Lord (if there is a Lord), save my soul (if there is a soul).*
>
> Joseph Renan (1823–1890)

However, maybe we should be grown-up about all this immortality: we're never going to be *really* immortal, are we?

> *Even were you about to live three thousand years or thrice ten thousand, nevertheless remember this, that no one loses any other life than this which he is living, nor lives any other than this which he is losing.*
>
> *The longest-lived and the soonest to die have an equal loss; for it is the present alone of which either will be deprived, since (as we saw) this is all he has and a man does not lose what he has not got.*
>
> The Meditations of Marcus Aurelius, AD 121–180

> *The man in a flutter for after-fame fails to picture to himself that each of those who remember him will himself also very shortly die, then again the man who succeeded him, until the whole remembrance is extinguished as it runs along a line of men who are kindled and then put out.*
>
> *And put the case that those who will remember never die, and the remembrance never dies; what is that to you? For now you are putting off unseasonably the gift of Nature, which does not depend on the testimony of someone else.*
>
> The Meditations of Marcus Aurelius, AD 121–180

> *Do not stand at my grave and weep –*
> *I am not there, I do not sleep.*
> *I am a thousand winds that blow;*
> *I am the diamond glints on snow.*
> *I am the sunlight on ripened grain;*
> *I am the gentle autumn's rain.*
> *When you awaken in the morning's hush,*

> *I am the swift uplifting rush*
> *Of quiet birds in circled flight*
> *I am the soft star that shines at night.*
> *Do not stand at my grave and cry,*
> *I am not there; I did not die.*
>
> Mahkah Native American Prayer

A good death

> *Spare me the whispering, crowded room,*
> *The friends who come, and gape, and go;*
> *The ceremonious air of gloom –*
> *All which makes death a hideous show.*
>
> Matthew Arnold, 'A Wish'

Good for whom? We have a vague concept of the 'good death'. It has something to do with the person having lived a long, fulfilling life, the death being expected and the person and their family being 'ready'.

They die, painlessly, in their sleep after an uneventful illness which requires no extended caring on the part of the family: all are mature and well-behaved; no complaints; no fuss.

Whilst this all seems to be about the dignity of the dying person, it is just as possible that talking about a 'good death' is a way of the survivors describing how well they – the family and friends – have survived the events leading up to and around the death.

Because of this confusion, it is probably just as well to avoid the phrase.

There are, however, some factors which have been found to contribute to a satisfactory (if not happy) death:

◆ It's important that the person involved has had a full and broad experience of life; they have had, and taken, opportunities, which have helped them grow and develop personally. They will have broadly achieved their aims in life.

◆ They should have had full and rich relationships, which have endured. A vital consequence of this is that feelings have been fully expressed and there is no 'unfinished business': everyone will be upset, but not because things have been left unsaid. All opportunities for saying 'goodbye' should have been offered and taken.

◆ The dying person should have been given the opportunity and resources to be 'in charge' during the closing stages of their lives, including the choice of place and company. They should have received adequate pain relief, if necessary, without it affecting their lucidity.

◆ They should have had the opportunity to set out their wishes for their funeral; their wishes for the disposal of their property should have been clearly (and legally) described.

The moral perspective

This is the background to most people's lives. Whichever culture or religious background we belong to, we tend to have common principles about how to live our lives and what sort of person we should aim to be as we approach death.

It may seem difficult to reconcile the apparently different ideas of all the world's religions (and even more so to include atheists as well), but there are common threads to do with 'proper' values, conduct and behaviour.

Most people have a sense of how they would like to lead their lives. Many draw inspiration from religious belief, many from humanist values. Generally, however, we are agreed that what we do 'matters'. It is rare to come across someone who sees their life as a pointless, negative business, who is careless of the approval of others and has no hopes for the future.

If we believe that what we do matters – because it shapes what we become – we will tend to have a positive attitude towards the challenges of life. These are the means by which we grow and develop.

Thus, at each different stage of life, we will seek to throw ourselves into the tasks and duties appropriate to it. In youth we will be serious about education and developing our talents; later we will become positively engaged in our careers and we can then extend our commitment to establishing a partner relationship and family or creating some other fulfilling pathway through our life.

There are also the widely held human values of 'right and wrong', 'honesty', 'integrity', 'justice', 'fairness' and 'goodness' which most people would subscribe to – although how they are interpreted will vary within and across cultures.

How far we measure up to these personal, social and, for some people religious aspirations will become important as we approach the close of our life. If we can believe that we've 'done our best' – that we've lived a 'good-enough' life – it will be easier for us to claim a 'good' death for ourselves.

This is an idea which is more usually associated with religious belief – with implications for some sort of meaning after death – but, in many ways, it is all the more important for the humanist for whom this is all the life there is.

To have lived as fully, completely and harmlessly as possible, to have made some contribution to the community and to have been important to others in some way are important considerations at the end of life.

It is difficult to imagine that someone who has squandered their abilities or who has consistently done harm to others and will be remembered positively by no one could have a 'good' death.

How can we lengthen our life span?

> *Life-expectancy is decreased by 15 minutes for every cigarette smoked. Since smoking a cigarette takes about 4 minutes, it's not worthwhile to smoke unless the smoker is more than four times as happy when they are smoking as when they are not smoking.*
>
> Linus Pauling, 1960

I assume we all know the dos and don'ts of good health care – be careful about nutrition, don't smoke, don't drink too much or take drugs. To have got this far in this book is proof of your good sense.

There are other ways to extend longevity that are more or less recommended with varying degrees of proof – vitamin supplements, vegetarianism, fasting, mineral waters, royal jelly, garlic, ginseng – as well as a list of various treatments and therapies which may or may not be successful.

There are, however, some other attitudes, behaviours or factors that have been positively and convincingly linked to increasing the number of our years.

'What's your recipe for a long life?'

This is the traditional interview question to the centenarian celebrating her (usually 'her') birthday. We never learn much from their replies but there have been studies of people who have reached 100 years. They have identified some common ingredients in the recipe.

What was striking about the centenarians in this research was not the fact that they had followed particularly healthy regimes – some of them were outstanding sinners – but their attitudes to life, their outlook and everyday lifestyle:

◆ They took a lot of mild exercise – not from an interest in health but out of enjoyment: country walks, gardening, dancing. They had never intentionally jogged or worked up a sweat: moderate amounts of ordinary exercise – but often.

◆ They had a tranquil, steady personality. They were reasonable, tolerant people, not given to strong expressions of emotion.

◆ They lived in pace with their age. They didn't try to cling to their past but got on with interests suited to their current state of maturity.

◆ They took a pride in their achievements. Not that they were particularly successful in the worldly sense, but they tried to make a good job of what they were doing. If they wanted to be a wife and mother they would have been very good at it: if they wanted to be a lawyer they would aim to be the best – not out of any considerations of competition or wealth, but for their own satisfaction.

◆ They were sociable. Although they were happy with their own company, they much preferred to be with other people – especially small groups where they could achieve deeper levels of contact. They were emotionally outgoing: they liked people.

◆ They were self-confident. They had a strong sense of self-esteem and were confident about who they were, what they did and what their values were. They trusted their own opinions and decisions and took responsibility for what they did. They did what is 'right' rather than what people expected them to do.

◆ They had a clear sense of purpose. They knew where they were going and gave a commitment to their actions.

◆ They were, in general, optimistic. They expected the best of other people and what the future might hold, but were not unrealistic. They kept themselves open to new experiences and change.

◆ They had a capacity to experience pleasure and deliberately to pursue the pleasures of life. They made space for fun and enjoyment in their life. If their pursuit of joy left them vulnerable to pain, it was worth it. They didn't 'play safe'.

◆ They showed the moderation that is advised for us all. However, in their case it had come naturally. They never needed the Health Education Authority to tell them that too much alcohol could be dangerous. If they smoked they didn't agonise about it. They 'never had time' to get fat.

◆ They had lived a life where everything was 'in its place'. Not that they were obsessive about tidiness or strict with their children: they knew who they were, what to expect from life and how to live it in an orderly, anxiety-free way.

◆ They didn't take themselves too seriously: they had a sense of humour and were tolerant of the shortcomings of other people.

◆ They tended to have been in long-term relationships within a family context. They felt part of a community and were accepted and acknowledged by others.

Does this sort of life sound familiar?

We're talking about people whose lives had been relatively free from stress. But how can absence of stress extend your life?

Our bodies work best when we're leading a normal, balanced, stable life. All the various systems get on with their job working in harmony with each other and the world outside; they each have their job to do and they do it well.

Our biology, however, was created for coping with a very different kind of environment; centuries ago we lived in less civilised times – more dangerous times when we might be victims to unexpected catastrophes from wild beasts and other people. Our bodies were made to deal with such dangers.

When we were challenged by some life-or-death situation we had only two choices: to face up to the threat or escape from it – fight or flight. Prehistoric people hadn't yet learned the sophisticated skills of 'sitting down and talking about it'.

What we urgently needed at such critical moments was:

♦ to be very quickly aware of the level of the danger
♦ to decide whether the best solution was to fight or flee
♦ to know how to do it.

We also needed to be able, urgently, to summon up a great store of energy to do the fighting or fleeing.

Over time the bodies of those who survived developed a biological system which helped them do this. Faced with danger, the body would automatically and speedily draw energy from those parts that, for the moment, didn't need it. This energy could then be channelled into the brain, for thinking and perception, and the major muscles, to prepare for action. The cave person would use this energy to great effect by attacking the beast or escaping.

Once the danger was past the energy would have been spent and all the biological systems would return to normal.

Nowadays, however, it is rarely considered appropriate to attack someone physically or run away when we are confronted by life's challenges – we like to think that we can work things out more sensibly. Our bodies, however, are still fitted with this old-fashioned 'fight or flight' facility.

When our boss or the bank manager bears down on us, the same biological system operates: energy is drawn from the non-essential (for the moment) parts of the body – e.g. the stomach, the digestive system, the liver, the kidneys, the reproductive system – and moved to the muscles, ready for action.

We rarely strike bosses and there's nowhere to run from bank managers, but our bodies haven't learned this yet. They provide us with the means to do both – and we do neither. Our muscles and brains remain primed for action and the rest of our body stays 'on hold'.

We can cope with minor, isolated challenging incidents and

the body eventually recovers from this false alarm. However, if the challenge is great enough or sustained over a period, or if we suffer from many challenging situations over a period of time, we begin to feel the effects.

The chemicals lodged in our muscles keep them in a state of tense readiness, our brains remain exercised and over-active and the deprivation of the rest of our system begins to take its toll in a variety of ways – ulcers, increased blood pressure, poor absorption of nutrients, impotence, fatigue, alcoholism.

Many people would also make links with a general weakening of the immune system leaving us more susceptible to life-damaging disease.

Think about things

> *Human life most nearly resembles iron. When you use it, it wears out. When you don't, rust consumes it.*
>
> Marcus Porcius Cato, (234–149 BC)

In 1998 at the University of Kentucky there was some research published which showed that an active imagination could lead to a longer life.

A study of elderly nuns showed that those who showed a more active mind in their youth lived significantly longer and were less likely to suffer from Alzheimer's disease.

The 180 nuns had all grown up together since their youth and were now in their late eighties: they had shared the same environment, had the same experiences and eaten the same food. When they took their vows almost 60 years earlier, they had written lengthy autobiographical essays. These were analysed by the researchers to assess their linguistic and thinking abilities: those who expressed the highest number of ideas were given the highest scores.

Since the beginning of the study, 58 of the nuns had died. The average death age of the nuns who had shown the lowest density of ideas in early life was 81.7 years. The more imaginative subjects lived for an average of 88.5 years.

The low-scoring thinkers in their youth were ten times more likely to develop Alzheimer's disease in old age. The average age at death of all the nuns was higher than in the general population.

One of the Sisters who took part in the study said (in the *Sunday Times*, May 1998):

> *Nobody ever seems to die young in our congregation. Most last well into their eighties or nineties....many of them read avidly, were engaged in local issues and enjoyed television quiz shows.*

You can live as long as you feel

In the 1970s a large study involving 3,000 Canadians who were all over 65 years looked at responses to the question: 'For your age would you say that your health is excellent, fair, good or poor?' (None had any immediately life-threatening diseases.)

The researchers checked their health records for the following six years. It was discovered that three times as many of the subjects had died who had answered 'poor' as those who had answered 'excellent'.

A similar study in Alameda County, amongst 7,000 mixed-aged Californians, asked the same question. At a follow-up after nine years it was found that the men who had answered 'poor' were twice as likely to be dead as the ones who had given an 'excellent' response: 'poor' women were five times as likely to be dead than 'excellent' ones.

It seemed that their negative perception of their well-being had a real effect.

A healthy mind in a healthy body

At Harvard University in 1979 there was some research on a group of 200 men that looked at the influence of their mental health on their general health from puberty and over the following 40 years. The study made allowances for other influences on longevity such as age of parents, weight or alcohol or tobacco use.

Of the 59 who had the best mental health between the ages of 21 and 46, only two became chronically ill or had died by the age of 53.

But of the 48 with the worst mental health between their twenties and their forties, 18 were dead or had suffered a chronic illness by their fifties. The director of the study, George Vaillant, concluded that the results:

> *showed that good mental health retards mid-life deterioration in physical health.*

Bad attitudes can be heartbreaking

At Duke University in North Carolina in 1981, a researcher came across a batch of psychological tests that a group of medical students had completed 25 years earlier. They traced 225 of the students – now doctors – and compared their present health against their teenage psychological profiles.

One finding was clear: those students who had a high test score for hostility and cynicism were five times more likely to have died in the meantime from coronary artery disease. (Again, the results were adjusted to exclude other possible causes.) Redford Williams, who directed the study, believes that:

> *Hostility has a direct effect on your coronary arteries. But, in addition, individuals who show an obvious dislike or avoidance of other people get disliked and avoided themselves. Belonging to a support network increases your chance of survival. Not belonging reduces it. So maybe these hostile doctors simply kicked away their life support systems.*

Church attenders can keep smoking

Russell Stannard from the Open University reported on BBC Radio 4's *Today* programme in May 1999 that research has revealed that regular (once a week) churchgoers, who have been life-long smokers, have the same life-expectancy as people who have never smoked.

Of course, it's not as simple as that. It's unlikely that there is any straightforward spiritual advantage in simple weekly worship. However, people with a settled religion are likely to be generally more thoughtful and reflective about their lives than others. Concern about their spiritual life is likely to be matched by concern for their health, relationships and other aspects of their day-to-day lives. So, even if you are an unbeliever, it's worth living your life as though you were. (You don't *have* to smoke as well, of course.)

Cut down on the calories

> *Man lives on one-quarter of what he eats.*
> *On the other three-quarters his doctor lives.*
>
> Inscription on a pyramid, 2000 BC

In the 1980s an American gerontologist, Ray Walford, following up on convincing animal research at the Cancer Research Institute in Philadelphia, advocated a '120-year diet'. This is based on the idea that if we restrict our daily intake of calories (1,800 for a man, 1,300 for a woman) our body's metabolism works more efficiently on less fuel. This optimum functioning protects our immune system from the wear and tear of normal ageing. (It's necessary, of course, to be extra careful about the nutritional balance of our food intake. It's also important to reduce our intake gradually over 5–7 years.)

It hasn't been possible to prove this theory, as users of the diet will have to complete their life spans before we really know. However, it is more than a theory: extensive, repeated research has been conducted in a variety of animal species which proves conclusively that 'undernutrition without malnutrition' has many beneficial effects: disease associated with ageing – cancer, cataracts, kidney and heart disease – is significantly reduced in animals on restricted diets.

Rats increased their normal lifespans (1,000–1,099 days) by over a half (1,600–1,699 days) on a calorie-restricted diet: this effect was also noted (proportionately) if the regime was begun in later life.

Make some good friends

It has been shown in much research that lack of social contacts with family or friends will increase our risk of disease.

In one American study of 5,000 men and women, the mortality rate was double for the men and triple for the women with the least social contact. Unattached men were most at risk. Newly widowed men died at a greater rate than married men of the same age – and this vulnerability continued for over a year after their partner's death.

However, although the loss of a relationship is potentially harmful, it is a 'one-off' and our immune system will recover. Continuing problems within a relationship are another matter: in another long-term study of 38 married women, those who were in difficult marriages were depressed and this reduced the efficiency of their immune systems over a period of many years exposing them to a much increased risk of life-threatening disease.

Sexual activity is also good for us. In 1997 the *British Medical Journal* published the results of the Caerphilly study which studied over 900 men. Those who had frequent orgasms (1–2 times a week) were 50 per cent less likely to die prematurely. Why (and whether it also applies to women) is not clear.

Sweat a few more years on to your life

Apart from the beneficial effect that exercise can have in reducing stress, it can also have life-extending effects on our lung-oxygen-heart-circulation-brain systems. Regular 20–30 minute bursts of activity three or four times a week can keep the circulation and muscles in good working order and extend their useful lives.

It's important, however, that this exercise should be steady, measured, and fairly intensive – without being over-strenuous. We should feel out of breath, but not so much that we couldn't carry on a conversation: there should be no pain or discomfort.

(We can't, however, seek even longer life by doing even more exercise: we're no better off running 100 miles a week than 20.)

Regular exercise of this sort also helps ensure healthy bone maintenance and prevent loss of calcium. It will help arrest osteoporosis which causes bone fragility and fractures. By the age of 65, 33 per cent of women will have some damage to their vertebrae and by the age of 81, 33 per cent of women and 18 per cent of men will have had a fractured hip – which can often lead to death.

A report in the *Independent* (July 1999) suggests that aerobic exercise also has an important part in developing and sustaining intelligence as we age (our friend oxygen again).

It's possible to overstate the effect of exercise on longevity – it may not add many years to our lives – but it will certainly help us have a healthier, fitter and happier old age.

Don't give up

Steven Greer studied women at the Royal Marsden Hospital who had had mastectomies following a diagnosis of breast cancer three months earlier. He divided them into four groups:

◆ *Women whom he described as having a 'fighting spirit':* they were determined not to succumb to the cancer and were determined to get better.

◆ *Some who showed denial of the seriousness of their condition:* 'they removed my breast as a precaution; everything's all right now.'

◆ *Others who revealed a stoic acceptance:* 'I know it's cancer but I've just got to carry on; we'll just have to see what happens.'

◆ *Another group who were the hardest hit.* For them their world was at an end and it was 'just a matter of time' before they were going to die.

These women were followed up for ten years to see if there was any connection between their attitudes and the outcome of the disease.

There was. Five years later the women in the first two of these groups were much more likely to be alive than women from the 'stoic' or 'hopeless' groups. Ten years later only 20 per cent of the 'hopeless' group had survived – but 80 per cent of the 'fighters' were still alive.

Whilst the optimism and hope of this research was encouraging, in recent years there has been an insidious backlash.

In her 1983 book, *You Can Heal Your Own Life* – which is still selling 300 copies a week – Louise L. Hay proposed that, such was the power of a positive attitude, those people who succumbed to cancer were responsible for allowing themselves to be too negative.

We have seen that people respond to terminal disease in

many ways. To imply that those who are incapable of assuming a 'fighting attitude' somehow then have to take the blame for their 'early' death seems cruel: it assumes they should have had the resources to change their personalities.

John Diamond, who has written about his own experience of throat cancer in his book *C: Because Cowards Get Cancer Too*, is quoted in the *Independent on Sunday* (July 1998):

> *I've known a number of people who died young of cancer, including a beloved sister-in-law and a dear aunt who had two young children. To suggest these women died because there was too much negativity surrounding them is a filthy suggestion....*
>
> *It would be nice to discover that the world was a just place where virtue was rewarded. In such a perfect world those who suffered cancer with a firm jaw and brave whistle would live, while those who hid under the bedclothes would be the ones who died....But that simply isn't how it is.*

Be more equal

We have seen earlier that life expectancy has been rising during the twentieth century by about two years each decade. If pushed to explain this, we would probably put it down to medical advances, better nutrition, improved public health and health education.

However, things are not that simple. The increase in longevity is heavily weighted towards those people in the more privileged social classes. There are some deprived parts of our large industrial cities where people can expect to live ten years less, on average, than their well-heeled neighbours in the leafy suburbs.

According to research studies, in comparison with the rich, the poor in Britain are more likely to die early from around 80 different diseases. These include cancers of the lung, heart disease, stroke, diabetes, bowel and stomach cancer, asthma and emphysema: there is also a higher incidence of infant death, accidents, Alzheimer's disease and depression.

In the 20 years up until 1970 there was a steep decline of 20 per cent in the death rates of men in the higher social classes –

lawyers, managers, doctors. When death rates were examined during the same period for men at the other end of the social scale – unskilled and semi-skilled workers – they were found to have remained fairly constant. The worst-off are nearly twice as likely to die substantially earlier than the best off. This is shocking. However, it's understandable: poor areas often lack good educational and medical facilities, housing and nutritional choice is limited by poor incomes. This must be true, but it is not, by far, the whole story.

In 1976 there was a fascinating study by a medical researcher, Michael Marmot, into heart-attack rates in Whitehall civil servants. These were not poor, disadvantaged people. However, there were clear differences in life expectancy within the group. This was related to social status. People in the lowest work grades were more at risk of heart attacks, strokes, some cancers and stomach diseases than their senior managers. The senior managers in turn were at greater risk than *their* bosses who ran the departments. You seemed to keep this life-span advantage even if you were a smoker or had high blood pressure. It seemed to be down to social and employment status. Describing this research in his book *Unhealthy Societies: The Afflictions of Inequality* in 1996, the economist Richard Wilkinson wrote:

> *If a virus or something toxic in the water were killing as many civil servants as the professional hierarchy seemed to be, the Whitehall buildings would be evacuated and closed down.*

He concludes that it isn't poverty as such which is the problem but *deprivation relative to other people*. The lower your income and the less independence and choice you have over your life and working conditions compared to others around you, the greater your risk of early death.

The best way to improve our life chances is not to increase everyone's resources but to narrow the immense differences in wealth and opportunities across our unequal society.

Richard Wilkinson even goes so far as to draw the amazing conclusion that taking away some of the wealth and power of the very rich could have the same life enhancing effect as raising the income and voice of the very poor.

A common sense of purpose, fellowship and shared ambitions within the community might be a better recipe for good health than economic equality. In April 1999, the National Heart Forum published research showing that deaths from heart disease in Britain were not falling as rapidly as in the United States or Australia – except for one section of the population: deaths of under-64s in social class one had dropped steeply.

> At the top of the social tree, people are less likely to smoke and more likely to eat their life-enhancing quota of five portions of fruit and vegetables a day.
>
> The Guardian, 28 April 1999

It's not only nutrition, however. Michael Marmot, Professor of Epidemiology and Public Health at University College, London, confirms the earlier research that stress is a major factor. The stereotype of the highly stressed business executive is wrong. People suffering the highest level of stress are to be found further *down* the social scale living in communities and working in jobs where they do not feel in control of their lives.

There was a study by the Office of National Statistics involving three million cancer patients over 25 years, published in the *British Journal of Cancer* (April 1999). Here it has emerged that if the death rates of well-heeled patients for all forms of cancer were reflected equally across the population, nearly 13,000 lives could be saved every year.

> I want to nail a myth. Cancer survival is not a lottery. Lotteries are fair. A ticket buys you the same chance of winning whether you are rich or poor and whether you live in Leeds or London.
>
> Professor Michael Coleman,
> London School of Hygiene and Tropical Medicine, 1999

Friends of the Earth published a report in May 1999, *Pollution Injustice*, revealing that one study of 27 poor estates on Teesside showed a link between industrial emissions and deaths from lung cancer. Eighty-six per cent of people disabled by asthma, which is aggravated by air pollution, come from the three lowest social classes. Children living in poor parts of Bristol have been shown to have twice as much lead in their blood as children from middle class areas.

Of the most polluting factories in England and Wales, only five are in areas where the average household income exceeds £30,000; 662 can be found in places where average incomes are less than £15,000 (*Independent on Sunday*, 9 May 1999).

It's a delicate area but there is hard statistical proof now that the more well-off we are:

◆ the better we eat and the better our general health: our bodies are more ready to fight disease
◆ the more educated and well-informed we are about health care: we are readier to seek help earlier
◆ the more able we are to attend hospital easily and to comply with treatment
◆ the more articulate and assertive we are about demanding the very best quality care from specialists rather than GPs.

The obvious good news for those of us who are poor is that none of the above factors is actually dependent on money. So long as we are careful, cautious, assertive and insistent we can live just as long by *pretending* to be rich.

If there is any truth in this (and which of us does not feel it in our bones?) what can we do to improve our life expectancy?

We can continue with what happens politically at present: some of us will work to create a more equal society by redistributing resources and giving more respect and value to people.

On the other hand, some of us can take the direct, headstrong route (much preferred by our genes) and strive to improve our position in society in competition with others. Hard effort will raise us to those heady social levels that might add at least a decade to our – and our successors' – lives.

Queen Elizabeth the Queen Mother is 99.

Get a good night's sleep

> *Early to rise and early to bed*
> *Makes a man healthy, wealthy and dead.*
>
> James Thurber, *New Yorker* 1939

The American Cancer Society conducted a massive survey involving over a million people to compare lifestyles with future health. One surprising result (which has been confirmed in other studies) was that people who slept six hours or less a night have their chances of dying over a period of nine years increased by 33 per cent.

Three characteristics of poor sleepers are anxiety, increased adrenaline production and increased body temperature. It's thought that there may be an underlying biochemical imbalance, which reduces the efficiency of their sleep.

Engage with life

No matter what we do, we're unlikely to add dozens of years to our life. Our genetic inheritance will usually determine that most of us will die well before our hundredth birthday. What we can do is to organise things so that we don't actually conspire with our genes to make things worse.

There are agreed ways of living 'properly' in a physical, social and spiritual sense which will guarantee – all things being equal – that we will live longer lives. If the increased years are few, we can at least ensure that what time we have will be less dogged by illness and infirmity.

The main secret seems to be to become *engaged* with life: to respect our bodies and each other: to delight in opportunities and to enjoy the experiences that life has to offer.

Many people's tombstones should read, Dead at 30; buried at 60.

Nicholas Murray Butler

We fear preparing for death and yet fear dying unprepared.
RICHARD SELZER

Getting Down To It

I t's all very well *thinking* about our deaths, but as we shall see, there are many things we can attend to now which will help settle our minds – particularly as what we do now can relieve a lot of the distress for our survivors.

Making your will

Most people see their affairs as straightforward: we're not wealthy and it's clear that everything we own will go to our partner after we die. In most cases this is true and there is no real need to make a will – except it will make things clearer and smoother after we've gone. Such automatic inheritance only applies:

- if we are married to our partner
- if we have no living children, parents or siblings
- and our property and money total less than £233,000.

Imagine you fell out with your parents thirty years ago and have since lived happily in an unmarried or a homosexual relationship – if you have not made a will, your parents will get everything. Fairness and moral rights don't come into it: the law lays down strict rules to do with inheritance.

People can always challenge anything that seems unfair – maybe successfully – but such post-mortem squabbles are unseemly and distressing.

What happens if there isn't a will?

In the case of someone dying intestate (without having made a will) the estate is divided up according to established rules:

- The widowed spouse gets most – up to £125,000 plus personal possessions and the rest goes to the children (the spouse may have to sell the family home to release the children's share).

- ◆ If there is no spouse everything is shared out between the children. However, if one of the children has already died their share goes to any children *they* might have had.
- ◆ If the deceased has no spouse, children or grandchildren, his estate goes to his parents: if no parents, his siblings. (Then nephews and nieces, grandparents, uncles and aunts: cousins are last in line.)
- ◆ Someone who has been supported by the intestate deceased and has lived with them for more than two years has a right to make a claim to the Chancery Court for 'reasonable provision' from the estate. This only applies to people who have lived together as 'man and wife': gay relationships are excluded but this may soon change.
- ◆ If you die without relatives or defendants, the whole of your estate goes to the Crown.

So, if you think you should have some say in the disposition of your hard-earned worldly goods, pick up the phone now. If you are anything other than married, childless and of modest means, you really must make a will: your survivors will thank you for spending the £50 it'll cost to have it done properly by a solicitor.

Writing your own will

Most people will tell you that you should always use a solicitor to draw up your will. Others – even some lawyers – will say that, if your wishes are simple and straightforward, you could do it yourself. If your situation is like the one described earlier – married, no young children and of modest means – you should be able to write your own will with the help of various aids obtainable from stationers.

The best sources of guidance are:

- ◆ The Which publication. *Make Your Will: a Practical Guide to Making your Own Will (England and Wales Only)*.
- ◆ Various books and materials from Law Pack Publishing covering wills and probate. Their website is at www.lawpack.co.uk.
- ◆ The Law Society's website at www.lawsociety.org.uk.

If any questions remain in your mind after reading the above, you almost certainly need to talk to a solicitor. This is particularly true when it comes to arrangements about children:

◆ Will your wishes be clear to others?
◆ Who would be their guardian?
◆ Are you really happy about your 18-year-old son being able to decide what to do when he inherits your £150,000 house?
◆ Do you want to have a view about what happens to your estate in the unfortunate event of the simultaneous death of yourself, your partner and your children?

Nobody is forcing you to have an opinion, but if you don't, you will have to accept that the law will make decisions that you might not have liked.

There is no reason why you should not include your wishes about your funeral or the disposal of your body. However, the curious thing is that you have no real say over what happens to this most personal of possessions: when you are dead your body is 'un-ownable' and you have no further rights in the matter of its disposal. However, your next of kin will want to take your wishes into account – but do let your wishes be known before then. Lack of clarity can lead to some unfortunate results.

> *Come for your inheritance and you may have to pay for the funeral.*
>
> Yiddish Proverb

Inheritance tax

Inheritance Tax will need to be paid on the total value of the estate above a certain amount – currently (1999) £233,000.

Most people may think that this will not affect them. However, by the time property, possessions and other assets are valued and insurance policies are paid out, many people might be surprised that their estate will exceed the exemption threshold.

This is a tax which is too complex to go into here, but if you think this might apply to you on your death it would be worth seeking financial advice now as there are ways of reducing the eventual burden if you act in time.

Apparently 96 per cent of estates are not liable to the tax – but somebody's got to be among the remaining 4 per cent. You can find out more from the booklet *Inheritance Tax – An Introduction* from the Capital Taxes Office, Minford House, Rockley Road, London W14 ODF. (Tel: (020) 7603 4622.

Quite separate from the tax advantages of making gifts of money and possessions before you die is the psychological advantage of making positive decisions about your worldly goods: you can choose how they are disposed of – and to whom. As someone is quoted as saying in Marie de Hennezel's book *Intimate Death*:

> *It's time for me to give the things I love to the people I love.*

Donating your organs after death

People with kidney disease have to wait, on average, two years until a suitable kidney becomes available for transplant. There were 847 operations in 1998 and a waiting list of 6,628 people.

The alternative to a transplant is to use a kidney dialysis machine, which acts in place of the kidneys in removing impurities from the blood. The total cost of dialysis over four years is £25,000–£30,000. The equivalent cost of a successful transplant is £4,000–£5,000. Moreover, regular dialysis is a miserable business whereas a transplant can give complete restoration of health.

Generally in Britain about 1,000 people die each year because there are no suitable organs available for transplant. More and more donors are needed as rejection problems are overcome and the operation becomes routine. Many people take some comfort that, following their death, their organs may be used for transplantation.

In 1998, 71 per cent of people said that they would be willing to let their kidneys be used in transplant operations after their death. The unhappy paradox, however, is that only 33 per cent had organ donation cards and only a disappointing 4 per cent carried their cards around with them regularly. A third of relatives will withhold their permission – even though it is not theirs to give, as nobody can 'possess' a body.

In Belgium you can register your wish *not* to be a donor at any town hall – this national register is consulted before any proposed organ removal. It's interesting that only 5 per cent of the population have chosen to opt out of donation – almost all on religious grounds. There has been a 37 per cent increase in successful transplants.

In Britain there is the NHS Organ Donor Register where you can register your wish to donate. There is no need to carry a card, but it's a helpful additional indication.

The first cornea was transplanted in 1905, the first successful kidney transplant was in 1954 and heart transplantation goes back to 1967; liver, lungs, pancreas, heart valves and bone can also be used. Recently a skin bank has been established to treat burn victims.

Now, 3,000 people a year are given a new lease of life through organ transplantation and 3,000 others have their eyesight restored. Many things need to match or be very close to ensure a successful transplant. Blood group, age and weight are all taken into account. For kidneys the most important factor is tissue type, which is much more complicated than blood grouping. The more accurate the match the better the chances of success.

There is a better chance of getting a very close match if both donor and recipient are of the same race. In addition, some ethnic groups are more likely to be prone to kidney disease of a type that produces kidney failure. It's important, therefore, to have donors from all races.

Having a medical condition doesn't necessarily prevent you from being a donor: a doctor will take the decision. Blood is taken from all potential donors and it's tested to rule out transmittable diseases and viruses such as HIV and hepatitis.

Ideally organs should come from men under 35 and women under 40 who are in intensive care units and who have no history of heart disease. Livers, hearts and lungs will normally come from younger donors but there is no upper age limit for kidneys, bones and corneas. There is no requirement that kidneys should come from someone on life support in a hospital so long as they are removed within an hour of death.

Organs and tissues can be preserved up to the following times after heart death:

Heart	6–8 hours	Heart valve	36 hours
Lung	12 hours	Liver	12–24 hours
Kidney	48–72 hours	Pancreas	12–24 hours
Cornea	24 hours	Bone	36 hours

...and if frozen:

Skin	up to 5 years	Tendons	up to 5 years
Knee cartilage	up to 5 years	Bone	up to 5 years
Veins	up to 5 years	Bone marrow	up to 3 years

Organs can only be removed if two senior doctors have carried out established and repeated tests to determine that the patient is 'brain-stem dead'. Brain-stem death is that state in which the brain has ceased to have any control over basic bodily functions – breathing, blood circulation, etc. One of the doctors must have been previously unconnected with the patient.

The trouble is that, because these functions are being performed by a life support system, the patient appears to be well, if unconscious, and relatives are sometimes reluctant to accept the fact of death.

Just after a death it is not usually foremost in the minds of friends and relatives to suggest what can seem like mutilation. The common, early disbelief of grief causes confusion in relatives:

> *You will be asked for your consent to use the organs of your son at a moment when you do not really understand how you think of him, so recent or imminent is his death... This is the worst time to decide...*
>
> Mary Warnock, *Independent on Sunday,* July 1999

Doctors are also hesitant to raise the issue with distressed survivors. A third of relatives will withhold their permission – even though it is not theirs to give. It is natural for doctors to wish to respect their feelings, but the result is that too many organs go untransplanted. (If someone has clearly signified their wish for organs to be transplanted, 99 per cent of relatives will go along with it.)

After the doctors agree that the patient is 'brain-stem dead' and permission has been given, the emphasis shifts from the interests of the patient to the interests of the potential recipient: the patient continues to be sustained on a ventilator. When the time is right from the recipient's point of view, the organ is removed and the ventilator is switched off. All this needs prior explanation and discussion between you and your relatives.

If you wish to have a 'Donorcard' and have your name added to the register, you can find application forms in libraries, Citizens' Advice Bureaux and doctors' surgery. Otherwise write to:

◆ UKTSSA, Fox Den Road, Stoke Gifford, Bristol BS12 6RR. Tel: (0117) 975 7575.

Donating your body for research

> *Small boy: 'Where do animals go when they die?'*
> *Small girl: 'All good animals go to heaven, but the bad ones*
> *go to the Natural History Museum.'*
>
> E. H. Shephard, 1929

> *Doctors are whippersnappers in ironed white coats*
> *Who spy up your rectums and look down your throats,*
> *And press you and poke you with sterilised tools*
> *And stab at solutions that pacify fools.*
> *I used to revere them and do what they said*
> *Till I learned what they learned on was already dead.*
>
> Gilda Radner, 'Untitled Poem', 1991

In Britain every year about 40 medical schools and colleges receive 700–800 bodies donated by their previous owners. There's an equal proportion of men and women and most are older people with an average age of 70 years.

Many people are deterred from donating their body because they think they might not be a particularly good enough specimen or they think they are too old. In fact the older the better.

A body that has been the subject of a post-mortem examination will already have been dissected and will therefore be unsuitable. The way to leave your body for research is to mention your decision in your will.

Often people leave the donation decision until quite late in life – perhaps after having had a spell in hospital:

Having something serious put right concentrates the mind wonderfully. People realise they are mortal and they ask themselves: 'What am I going to do with my body when I die?'
Dr Laurence Martin, Her Majesty's Inspector of Anatomy

If the death has been reported to the coroner, his consent will be required. Often relatives wish to have a memorial service following the death in place of a funeral. A body may be kept for medical teaching purposes for up to three years. The medical schools will arrange and pay for a simple funeral, or the relatives can do this themselves. The medical school will advise relatives when the body is available for a funeral.

If you want to find out more about body donation after death, contact:

◆ *England and Wales* – HM Inspector of Anatomy. Tel: (020) 7972 4342.
◆ *Northern Ireland* – Department of Anatomy, Queen's University, Medical Biology Centre, 97 Lisburne Road, Belfast BT9 7BL. Tel: (01232) 29241 ext. 2106.
◆ *Scotland* – Departments of Anatomy, Universities of Aberdeen, St Andrews, Glasgow, Dundee or Edinburgh.

Advance directives: living wills

*O! let him pass; he hatest him
That would upon the rack of this tough world
Stretch him out longer.*

Shakespeare, *King Lear*

One way that you can have some control over how you are treated in certain life-threatening situations is to write an advance directive (sometimes called a living will). This anticipates the possibility that you might suffer a serious emergency, without consciousness. An advance directive gives you the opportunity of making your wishes known to your family and doctors about what you would wish them to do in particular circumstances.

It is less well known that a directive can be useful in less dramatic health care circumstances; for example, if I became moderately injured and temporarily unconscious – it's not a life or death matter – I would like it to be known that I don't wish to be fed certain foods.

The advance directive's use reflects developments in technology, which have dramatically improved our ability to prolong life – even though the quality of our life may become seriously diminished.

Just as, when conscious, we have the right to refuse any medical treatment, so, when unconscious, we have the same right.

We can use an advance directive, when our mind is conscious and clear, to assert our right to refuse a life-saving operation. The High Court, in 1993, agreed that we have the right to state in advance that we do not wish to accept a particular form of medical treatment.

This should not in any sense be confused with assisted death. (You cannot give an advance instruction for active steps to be taken for your life to be taken.) It is rather to do with whether we wish doctors to *intervene* or not to keep us alive. We cannot ask a doctor to do anything that is illegal or against good medical practice.

However, there are snags. Although we have the right to state our wishes and a doctor has a duty to pay attention to them, we're not going to be in a very good position to argue. Doctors are used to keeping people alive: they may be unsure of just how disabled we might become: they may think we're being pessimistic or unreasonable. When the crisis comes their inclination may be to take the survival option.

This is likely to be the case if we leave over-simple, unhelpful instructions such as:

- ◆ 'I do not wish to be a burden to my family.'
- ◆ 'I do not wish to suffer a lot of pain.'
- ◆ 'I do not want to be resuscitated if it means that my quality of life will be affected and I wish to avoid any loss of dignity.'

Such statements are vague and unspecific and no doctor is

going to guess at what a 'burden', a 'lot', 'quality of life' or 'loss of dignity' means.

◆ We need to give a full account of the background to our wishes.
◆ What are the precise circumstances where we wish to refuse treatment?
◆ What are the things in life that we value and what, in particular, would make our continuing life intolerable?

What do you want treatment to accomplish? Is it enough that treatment could prolong your life, whatever your quality of life? Or, if life-sustaining treatment could not restore consciousness or your ability to communicate with family members or friends, would you rather stop treatment? Once you have stated your goals for treatment, your family and physicians can make medical decisions for you on the basis of your goals. If treatment would help achieve one of your goals, it would be provided. If treatment would not help achieve one of your goals, it would *not* be provided.

You should also show in your statement that you have given full consideration to the alternatives and that you have informed yourself about the full range of medical treatments and community services which might be thought to make your continuing life acceptable. It would be helpful to anticipate possible scenarios and make clear, in principle, how you would want to be treated in each one.

The clearer a picture you can leave for doctors and family about how you would be likely to view any proposed treatment in your unconsciousness, the more confident they will feel that they are doing what you want rather than making crucial decisions themselves on your behalf. This clarity can be emphasised by discussing your wishes with your doctor and family in advance so they can have a clearer idea of what is in your mind and how sure your intentions are.

You should, of course, make sure that your doctor and family have copies of the document. An advance directive is not something to be left until the last moment. The sorts of medical emergencies in which your wishes need to be known are as likely to happen in your twenties as your eighties.

Because you may wish to formally declare your wishes decades before the directive may be needed, it is important to update, re-sign and have it witnessed regularly – say every year. In some US states there is an 'expiry limit' of 5 or 7 years. You may wish to redraft the statement occasionally. You may even decide that the whole thing is a bad idea: in which case, make sure that all copies are retrieved and destroyed.

An advance directive has legal force:

◆ If you were mentally capable of making decisions when you drew it up.
◆ If you intended that it should apply in the situation that later arose and knew what the consequences of your decisions would be.
◆ If you have foreseen the circumstances and there is no reason to believe that you would have changed your mind.
◆ If the decision was yours alone, and was not made under anyone else's influence.

An alternative is to take out an Enduring Power of Attorney (see your solicitor) which allows you to nominate someone to make decisions on your behalf. Usually this is to do with handling money and business matters, but it can be applied to health care decisions. In October 1999 a Government White Paper has proposed that we should have a right to appoint someone to make decisions on our behalf.

In 1976, California was the first state to pass a law allowing advance directives and now every state has legislation in place: it's estimated that 20 million Americans have one. In America, there is even legislation to oblige all people admitted to residential care homes and hospitals to be informed of their right to make an advance directive.

Even if you're not sure if you want to go all the way, it's a salutary exercise to try to put your thoughts on paper – it's often only when you have to put something into words that you begin to formulate what your wishes might be.

For more detailed advice about drawing up your own advance directive, the Voluntary Euthanasia Society – Scotland, has a 'Living Will Pack'. Their address is:

Voluntary Euthanasia Society – Scotland, 17 Hart Street, Edinburgh EHI 3R. Tel: (0131) 556 4404.

Other organisations who can give further information and sample documents are:

♦ Voluntary Euthanasia Society (England & Wales), 13 Prince of Wales Terrace, London W8 5PG. Tel: (020) 7937 7770. Email. ves.london@dial.pipex.com

♦ British Humanists' Society, 14 Lamb's Conduit Passage, London WC1R 4RH. Tel: (020) 7430 0908.

A set of advance directives for personal use, including instructions and a medical emergency card, can be bought by non-members of these organisations.

It's estimated (I don't know how) that between 10 and 30 per cent of us in the UK have made an advanced directive.

The anticipated death

> *When I go, I want to die like my father, peacefully in his sleep. Not screaming in terror, like his passengers.*
>
> Bob Monkhouse, 1998

Many illnesses have two aspects that provide a challenge to their victim and their family: certainty of death and uncertainty of when it will take place.

An 'ordinary' death – following pneumonia or a heart attack, for example, where a person has been reasonably fit, becomes ill and dies within a week or so – is quite different from a death resulting from cancer, multiple sclerosis, AIDS or Alzheimer's disease. Here the terminal outcome is known but whether it will be in months or years remains uncertain.

Many of these conditions are degenerative and can cause profound changes in abilities, appearance and behaviour. The family of someone who has died following several years of dementia may well say 'For us, our mother died years ago.'

This 'social' or 'family' death can be very difficult to deal with. The changes are often subtle and there may well be times when 'she becomes her old self again'. The physical presence confuses the fact that the family have, effectively, 'lost' their mother. The important, remembered things about her, however, are rarely, if ever, seen: her sense of humour, her authority and wisdom, her pastry-making and good temper.

Growing physical and emotional dependence on children reverses the normal parent/child roles. Often, people think that time will help them get used to the prospect of death: this is not necessarily so. There has been some research that shows that bereavement is harder and longer for people who have cared for the dying person over a prolonged period.

If the final illness lasted for more than a year, the structures of the carers' lives were often disrupted; there had been opportunities for dashed hopes and disappointments; the guilt and exhaustion for all concerned may well have resulted in tension and bitter words.

If things are 'drawn out', the dying person will be able to observe the reactions of those around them to their dying: they may wonder whether their family are 'sad enough'; they may well correctly notice that people are distancing themselves and avoiding the subject of death – which is probably the subject which is uppermost in their minds.

Unfinished business

> Before her death my sister asked to see each of her five brothers and sisters. We talked about how we had been close and trusting with each other, and we also talked about some of our long-standing fights and grudges. I know that the hour she and I spent going over our times together was very important to me. It was one way to say goodbye. And I think it was important and healing for her as well.
>
> Quoted in *Ourselves: Growing Older*, J. Shapiro, 1989

As we go through life we learn to play a series of roles. Our parents and friends form our basic 'character' in childhood and youth but we gradually develop a series of variations that we can use – like suits of clothes – according to the occasion and the company. Our 'performance' at work will be different from how we behave with our children.

The mature adult will be aware of this role-playing and will keep in touch with her underlying identity. She will also 'speak' to the common humanness of other people, recognising that, however differently we seem to behave, we share common needs, feelings and motivations. In this way, members of a civilised society seek to understand and support each other, picking up problems and co-operating to solve them.

All of us sometimes make mistakes:

◆ We may hold on to our 'parent' role longer than appropriate so that we maintain a sense of 'power' over our children which overshadows family relationships.

◆ We may fail to grow out of our 'rebellious teenage' role and continue, for no apparent reason, to challenge authority wherever we meet it, puzzling those around us.

◆ We may go too far in taking on a 'respectable citizen' role: those around us will be careful of what they say for fear of upsetting us.

◆ Some of us will be destined never to grow out of our 'little girl/boy' roles and we will constantly be drawn to people who will 'look after' us.

None of us has only one role and we can measure our competence as adults by our flexibility in moving from one to the other, or in casting off old ones or developing new ones.

We can also play many roles within a single relationship according to the situation: long-term partners will know how, in different situations, it is possible for either of them to be strong, submissive, dominant, nurturing, selfish, kind, loving or aggressive.

Maturity is the ability to recognise that we are in charge of these facets of our behaviour and we can account for their expression. If we cannot be flexible we may become locked into a way of thinking or behaving which takes us over:

◆ A 'domineering' person becomes so stuck in their role at work that they gradually become incapable of praising their employees or delegating work to develop their staff's independence.

◆ A 'capable' person is so strongly defined by their 'victim' partner that they eventually become incapable of expressing their need for help.

◆ A 'tough' father and 'ambitious' son become so set in their ways that they lose the capacity to talk about their warm feelings for each other.

◆ A 'put-down' daughter has got so used to her role as a

'sufferer' that she can no longer be open about her feelings with her 'critical' mother.

◆ 'Competitive' sisters have become so used to their 'rivalry' roles that they lose sight of how much they have in common.

◆ 'Jealous' brothers lose their ability to acknowledge each other's achievements.

We usually find ways of living alongside each other fairly happily in this way, but when death appears on the horizon – our own or someone else's – things begin to get serious.

Death is for grown-ups: if there is to be a satisfactory leave-taking we need to cut through the role-playing to achieve clear, direct and honest communication:

Case study: Philip and Steven

Philip had been an only child and had always said that when he grew up he would have lots of children. He married Julie and within two years they had a son – Steven.

After a further 16 years Philip was forced to face the fact that there were not going to be any more children. However, one day he would be a grandfather – how many grandchildren would he have?

When he was 17, Steven told his parents that he was gay. Philip was devastated. From then on he gradually gave up his hopes for grandchildren and, although he seemed to accept Steven's homosexuality, quietly grew to resent his son's 'decision'. Steven thought his father was 'disgusted' by his homosexuality and began to avoid him. Their relationship cooled over the years. Steven went off to work successfully as an actor in the United States.

Julie died of breast cancer, Philip re-married and had three more children. His earlier obsession with being a grandparent declined but his coolness continued towards Steven on his rare visits home. Steven continued to be wary of his father's 'disapproval of his immorality'.

Both father and son had formed attitudes towards each other decades earlier, which were based on unreliable information. However, because there was no open discussion between them of their feelings, their relationship became stuck. Each one's coolness was nourished by the other's: they were uncomfortable but didn't quite know why.

When Philip had his first heart attack, Steven flew home the next day. As they talked in the hospital they each longed to recapture the father/son closeness that there had once been. But they couldn't do it.

Philip longed to tell Steven how proud he was of his success. Steven yearned to tell Philip how good a father he had once been. Both wanted to be 'accepted' by the other._____

How could this father and son have unravelled this situation?

Solution one: 'just do it'

This will be easier the more motivated they both are and the more urgent the situation. It will be much easier for them to do than either of them think – it's simply a question of steering the discussion into the appropriate area. It's worth rehearsing a selection of opening lines:

◆ 'Can I talk to you about something that has been on my mind for years?'
◆ 'I think it's probably time that we cleared the air between us....'
◆ 'Do you remember that day all those years ago when you said... and my response was...well....'
◆ 'We've never really had much opportunity to talk seriously with each other in the last few years....'
◆ 'I'm very bad at putting my feelings into words and sometimes people get the wrong impression of me....'

Usually, the other person is just as anxious to clear the air as we are and they will encourage and support such tentative openings: the rest of the conversation will be easier as we go on – especially if we continue to look for honest feelings, accepting responsibilities and avoiding recriminations.

We could spend some time imagining the conversation – trying to anticipate a 'script' which will enable rather than hinder the other person. What can we say which will care for any guilt or defensive feelings they might have? What can we say that shows we are looking for an improvement in our relationship and not looking to allocate blame? It's worth using actual spoken words in a private rehearsal.

Solution two: write it down

Dear Lea, my life is almost over. Before I go, I would like you to know that I no longer bear you any grudge. I am going in peace, and I hope you are at peace too. Please do not try to see me. Things are as they should be.

Quoted by Marie de Hennezel, *Intimate Death*

If you think that it is impossible for you to talk to the other person, try explaining yourself on paper. This has the advantage of clarity – you can say what you like without embarrassment and you can make sure it is clear. Open with an explanation:

This is going to be a difficult letter for me to write as I'm not very used to talking about my feelings, as you know. I have often wanted to talk to you about this over the last few years but there never seemed to be a proper time.

However, I think that we need to clear the air about something that has been on both our minds for some time. Life's too short for us to have drifted apart in this way and I want to make things as good between us as they once were.

Writing things down is often useful in any case. Often we know we have a problem about something but it is only when we have to find the exact words to express it that the problem itself becomes more focused and clear.

Solution three: get help

Often, when we find expressing feelings difficult, it is much easier if we have a third party to help. Just explaining things and answering questions makes a solution more possible.

It may be that a third person would be willing to sound out the other person or facilitate a three-way discussion. This can be very informal – the third person is there to enable the others to talk – nothing else.

Solution four: counselling

Talking on our own to a professional counsellor might throw some further light on the origins of the problem and why it is so difficult to discuss: we can also work out how we might go about raising discussion with the other person.

We may, in some circumstances, wish to ask a counsellor to arrange a meeting with both of us, if we feel that neither of us is up to working out a solution.

Solution five: act it out

It may be impossible for you to meet together to 'finish the business'. Nevertheless, have a 'reasonable' imagined conversation with the other person.

Imagine them sitting in a chair opposite you: imagine you are both in the best of moods – full of goodwill towards each other. Talk to the imagined 'other', explaining your feelings and acknowledging their sensitivities: go out of your way not to be hurtful. Imagine their positive response to what you have to say. Try to see each other's point of view – changing chairs and speaking aloud – it sounds odd, but the imagination can deliver some surprising feedback on reality.

How long have I got, doctor?

The actual uncertainty of the course and length of the illness may be made worse by doctors' use of language. In the 'Death and Dying' course from the Open University, a survey asked a group of doctors to express words to choose a definition for the word 'likelihood'. They were given a choice of nine definitions and asked to rate each one as an accurate definition. The results were:

Rarely	5 per cent
Commonly	75 per cent
A real chance	60 per cent
Typically	80 per cent
Invariably	95 per cent
Often	62 per cent
A small chance	8 per cent
Not usually	17 per cent
Not infrequently	45 per cent

These percentages were the average of everyone's score. The point of the exercise is to reveal the wide variation between the participants. One doctor thought 'likelihood' could only be defined as 'a real chance' 1 per cent of the time; another thought it could mean this level of certainty 99 per cent of the time.

What does our doctor mean when she tells us 'there's a real chance you'll be better by Monday'? Faced with all this uncertainty we may well, as patients, opt for the gloomiest prognosis – we are definitely going to die. And soon.

It may be that we are faced with a doctor who genuinely is uncertain about what to expect. It may be, however, that she thinks she is protecting us from the pain of knowing the truth. It may be that we wish to be protected in this way and her judgement is correct.

More likely, though, we wish to know the truth. In these circumstances we may find ourselves in the odd situation of being forced to give reassurance to our doctor that, if it is to be known, we really *do* prefer to know the truth.

The diagnosis of a terminal condition can be a fertile ground for deceit and halftruths. Apprehensive and uncertain health-care staff may conspire with patient and family to prevent themselves and each other feeling bad.

Information and expectations are often confused and muddled. In a survey of elderly widowed people, one-third said they had not been able to find out all they wanted to know about their spouse's illness. However, it was interesting that within the same group only 10 per cent said that they would have liked to have talked, or talked more, about the illness and what was likely to happen.

But he mustn't be told...

> *'Doctor, Doctor, shall I die?'*
> *'Yes, my child, and so shall I.'*
>
> Anon

If you had a disease which had been clearly diagnosed as terminal, would you like to be told? If you would prefer to be kept in ignorance, imagine what this would mean:

◆ You would have to ignore the fact that you were becoming

more and more frail and that no further positive treatment
was being offered.

◆ You would have to expect your doctors to lie to you and to
give you hope of a recovery.

◆ You would need to be insensitive to the anxiety and sadness
of your visitors.

◆ You would wish your doctor to deny the seriousness of your
illness to your relatives.

◆ You would expect them to conspire with you to make plans
for when you were better.

◆ You would wish to deny your loved ones the opportunity to
say goodbye.

◆ You would wish to deny yourself the opportunity to put
your affairs and your relationships in order.

It's hard to believe that anyone would wish such a scenario to
be played out around them. It's also hard to believe that
anyone could successfully fool themselves into such deliberate
and complete ignorance.

You would inevitably be aware of the vagueness of the
doctor, the profoundly changed attitude of your relatives and
your inner sense that there was something different about this
illness.

To view the situation from a relative's point of view, would
you really wish to conceal the truth from someone with a
terminal disease?

◆ Are you prepared to bring in holiday brochures to make
plans for when they are 'on their feet' again ?

◆ Are you willing to watch them become weaker and keep up
a pretence of hope?

◆ Are you really content for the end to come unacknowledged,
with no goodbyes?

◆ Will you tell his dearly loved sister not to come over from
Australia because 'he might be suspicious'?

I can imagine the patient and the relative both being terrified
and unwilling to face up to the fact. I can imagine them both
wanting to talk about it as little as possible; but not to know..?

Imagine the loneliness and isolation of suspecting – for you surely would – that you were dying. Not only that but everyone around you would seem overwhelmed to the degree that they could not bear to talk about it. How could you upset them further by raising the subject? You might well think the worst – 'maybe it's a matter of days or weeks' – when you really have several months left. You may fantasise about a final agony when you could be reassured about how any suffering could be reduced.

If you are a relative, it is not acceptable that a doctor should tell you of a terminal prognosis without having told the patient first and received permission for you to be told. However close your relationship, their confidentiality should be respected.

Many doctors find it as difficult as us to face up to mortality and sometimes they want to pass on to us the burden of breaking the bad news. This should be resisted. It is only the doctor who can talk with authority to his patient about their illness.

This is not to say that we should expect doctors to be immediately open and direct:

I'm afraid Mr Brown that there's nothing further that we can do for you – your condition will not improve and you must be prepared for the worst; we can hope for about six months.

This would be insensitive: it would also be inaccurate – things are never as cut and dried. A good doctor will judge how receptive his patient is likely to be and will lead the conversation in such a way as to encourage the patient to take the initiative to find out more at their own pace.

'The outlook isn't good' is hardly a death sentence, but it will set the scene for further enquiry if the patient wishes. If not, things can be left there. If they feel comfortable about asking the doctor specific questions, they will. If they are so blocked about facing the reality of their death, so be it. At least they can have 'what-if the-worst-comes-to-the-worst' conversations with their families which, although unsatisfactory, will open some avenues of honesty.

It is intolerable for everyone for the dying patient to be told that 'there's a good chance that you will get better.' This is a direct message to the patient to 'shut up'.

It is also unhelpful to relatives to be encouraged in any pretence – their future confidence in any medical reassurance on their own account will be severely dented.

If any of the parties – doctor, patient or relative – feels they have been caught up in a conspiracy of avoidance it might be useful for them to talk to someone outside 'the web' – a stranger, a social worker, a counsellor – to whom they might feel able to talk without any emotional overtones.

98 per cent of the people wanted to know they were dying.
60 per cent of doctors did not want to tell them.
80 per cent of people knew anyway.
Elizabeth Kübler-Ross, *On Death and Dying*

The near death experience

This curious phenomenon has emerged in recent years. There has always been some evidence about near-death experiences, but it is only since resuscitation techniques have become more sophisticated that their credibility has been established (more people recover these days to tell the tale).

There is little doubt that such experiences are common – if not usual. The puzzle continues about the cause. What is established is that people at the extreme point of death, just before being resuscitated, report a characteristic, changed state of consciousness.

It is likely that, at such a serious life-crisis, there should be a breakdown in normal thought processes. What is remarkable, however, is that, on the evidence of many independent reports, across a wide range of cultures and religions, these experiences are markedly consistent in their content.

What is even more compelling is the effect these experiences have afterwards on the surviving subject. The reports are not identical but they have many features that are very common:

◆ There is a distinct awareness of being separate from your body, watching the proceedings – hovering over them – as doctors and nurses attempt to revive you.

◆ There is an intense feeling of euphoria and well-being. Pain disappears.

- There is a sensation of being alone in intense darkness travelling a path, or a tunnel, which leads to a vivid brightness.
- You are convinced that when you reach your destination you will never return.
- Some episodes are reported as being evidently set in beautiful country scenery suffused with bright, rich colours and warm sunlight. On the other hand, there are opposite reports described in terms of a fearful nightmare within a grim, hostile environment.
- Many report what is a common experience for people in less extreme crises: 'my whole life passed before my eyes.'
- You may 'meet' with dead relatives and friends.
- Ophthalmologists report that people with lifelong total blindness say that they were able to see the activity around them – giving inexplicably graphic descriptions of the scene.
- Many people have spiritual experiences in line with their religious beliefs.
- The most striking effect, however, is that far from inducing the extreme terror you would expect, this is all experienced, almost universally, with a deep sense of tranquillity and relief.
- This all has a marked effect on your subsequent state of mind. Anxieties are reduced and, because you have 'experienced' it, any fear of death is lessened. It will strengthen religious beliefs and sustain (or create) a certainty about 'life after death'.
- It also seems to generate an empathy and love for other people. You will be keen to talk about what has happened and, in particular, there is a wish to share your new-found assurance with other people who may be approaching death.

At first we may be dubious about these reports of near-death experiences. They remind us of ghost stories, 'supernatural' events and science fiction – which most of us have come to disbelieve. There are also unfortunate associations with an immature conception of what 'heaven' might be like.

There's also no shortage of 'natural' explanations. In his book *The Way We Die* Leslie Ivan has been able to explain effectively all the reported accounts in terms of what is

happening in the dying brain following the failure of the
oxygen supply and the subsequent build-up of carbon dioxide.
There are chemical effects, which mirror the action of
tranquillisers, anti-depressants and hallucinogenic drugs.

However, there is evidence that these experiences are not
wholly accounted for by neurological and chemical changes.
The survivors' subsequent assurance and tranquil acceptance of
death remain unexplained.

There is, undoubtedly, more to know....

Your deathbed scene

> *When some old friend shall step to my bedside,*
> *Touch my chill face, and thence shall gently slide,*
> *And when his next companions say,*
> *'How does he do? What hopes?' shall turn away,*
> *Answering only with a lift-up hand,*
> *Who can his fate withstand?*
> *Then shall a gasp or two do more*
> *Than e'er my rhetoric could before,*
> *Persuade the peevish world to trouble me no more?*
>
> Thomas Flatman (1637–88), 'Death'

Where?

Do you want the medical security of a hospital ward (but with
the limits of access this gives you to people you might want
round you)? Or do you want the emotional security of your
own bed at home (with its medical limitations and heightened
emotional pressures)? What about the specialised, but explicit,
ambience of a hospice?

Do you want to live as long as possible or be as
comfortable as possible? It's for you to decide what your
priorities are and where these can best be found.

Who?

It's assumed that the saddest way to go is to die alone. Most
people will want to be with those who are closest to them
when they die: does this mean your partner and children, or do

you include your parents and your grandchildren?

What about the person you've been having a secret affair with for the last fifteen years whom you were travelling to meet when you had the accident?

Some people will prefer not to be the centre of a 'deathbed scene'. They will want to be allowed, after saying their goodbyes, to slip away quietly without ceremony.

How far should you be selfish about your death attendants and how much should you respect the wishes of others? It's for you to decide and it's for you to make your feelings clear.

How?

It's important to some people that they retain as much control over their life as possible until their last moments. They will have a lively interest in the likely impact of their death and they will want to tie up loose ends.

You may think that this is not the right time to start putting your affairs into order – you will read elsewhere in this book about how you could have done this better, earlier.

We all value honesty: it may be that there have been uncomfortable or hurtful things that have remained unforgiven for years. We may feel a wish to 'get things off our chest' before we go. Only we can judge the effect this might have: some may wish to open up complex discussion about past events – we will need to judge whether this will be wise at such a time: it's probably prudent to try to be positive.

There is no reason why we should feel the need to hold on to our control of things. Maybe you prefer to relax, let things take their course and allow those around you to be in charge – it may be a kindness to them.

What to say to people who are dying

What you can really do for a person who is dying, is to 'die' with him.

Dr K. R. Eisler

The first rule is that there are no rules. Each of us is different and all dying people will have different needs. We should be ourselves and treat them as the person we have always known.

Our first thought is that they are 'vulnerable victims' who need 'careful handling' and that we must be 'careful what we say'. We may try to rehearse comments and questions which will neither embarrass nor upset. It's hard, but such sensitivity may be misplaced and may interfere with direct communication.

Remember that they are likely to be fully aware of their situation and will be relieved that someone is willing to share their thoughts, anxieties and feelings.

Imagine dying surrounded by people who are avoiding the only subject on your mind: think what it would be like to have to be responsible for helping their embarrassment in addition to preparing for your own death.

On the other hand, we should be sensitive to people who clearly do not wish to talk. We may know that honesty and openness are recommended but this is not the time for psychological advice to the dying.

We will be sad to see the plight of someone so changed and with so little life left: we will want to express our feelings and show our sympathy. There is a danger that this will steer things round to us being the subject of the conversation when we really want the focus to be on them.

In our imagination we will have an idea about how we would react in their situation and we may want to tell them that we understand what they are feeling. However, we can never fully know what these last days mean to them and to imply otherwise may be curiously disabling, as if to say, 'I don't need to hear what you have to say because I already know – and look how well I'm dealing with it.'

Showing empathy, rather than 'sympathy', can be helpful. This is when you try to put yourself alongside them and try to see how things look from their point of view: this may encourage them to talk about how they feel.

On the other hand, our honest response to the situation may be appropriate. For example, we may be feeling awkward and at a loss for words. Rather than stumble on with banal small talk, it would be better to say something like: 'I know that there's so much to say but I feel at a loss for words. I'm gabbling on talking about me when it's you I came to see.'

We sometimes think that we've got to keep the

conversation going – that communication is 'words'. And yet we all know how powerful a quiet silence can be – silent talk. Also we know how comforting a gently held hand can be.

If we can find the strength, we have a responsibility sometimes for helping a dying person to talk about things that we know are important to them. We may also know that they may be sensitive about mentioning them for fear of hurting our feelings:

- ◆ Would they like to see their ex-partner?
- ◆ Did they mean it all those years ago when they said they wanted no funeral service?
- ◆ Do they want to change anything in their will?
- ◆ What should we do with their much-loved record collection?

There may be many things, which we know they might have an opinion about, and some things that we will be left to decide on our own when they are gone. It may be up to us to take a gentle initiative now rather than regret it when it's too late. It's important, however, that we don't put any pressure on them.

They should have the final privilege of being in charge of their own dying. It may even happen that there are things which they prefer not to share with us but which they want to talk about with someone else – a stranger even: we all have inner fears and needs which we are not used to discussing with our nearest and dearest.

It is also possible that the dying person, in death as in life, will not wish to be the focus of much talk and attention; they may wish to 'just slip away'. We may find this painful and rejecting, but so long as we make it clear that we are 'there' if they want us we should respect their wishes.

We so want to get these last conversations 'right' and yet it is not surprising that they will be difficult. We rarely experience such serious losses in our life and our performance is hampered by the inevitable jumble of grief and regrets that we are feeling.

We're sometimes likely to say the wrong thing. This is less likely if we try to be honest and open and if we show ourselves 'available' to their wishes. We should try – hard though it might be – to put our own need to grieve to one side. We shall soon enough have a lifetime for that.

Of course, if we could all be honest with each other and ourselves throughout our lives much of this awkwardness and uncertainty could be avoided. If we are less reticent about death with each other now, we can anticipate how our death might change things and we will not leave our partners guessing and regretting so much.

But I was speaking to her only this morning...

> *The sad part is that she died alone. There were no last 'I love yous', or 'thank yous', or 'Hey, I really appreciate all you dos'. There were no soft smiles, no caring words – only screams. Screams that echoed through the empty chambers of my mind where laughter once reigned.*
>
> Unattributed

Sudden death is the greatest test of our anticipation of mortality. For our life to end without any notice for us or those we leave behind is cruel and disastrous. And yet curiously most people see it as an enviable way out:

> *'I just want to slip away quietly in my sleep.'*
> *'He had a heart attack just after he won the golf tournament – what a way to go!'*

I suppose that we think we can avoid having to know that the end is near: we won't have to put our relatives through all the worry of having to cope with our dying. It was not always the case. In the distant past people longed for time to prepare for their dying: to go unexpectedly was the worst thing that could befall you. Mediaeval Christians believed it was a punishment for some offence – the sign of a wrathful God.

The truth is that some of the worst bereavement experiences follow a sudden death:

- ◆ The shock to our families can have severe, long-lasting effects.
- ◆ There can be much upsetting unfinished business.
- ◆ We are cheated of 'goodbye' opportunities.

In particular, parents of children who suffer accidental death and young widows may never fully recover – such is the force of the unexpected upset. We cope better when we are able to take things one step at a time.

The physical effects of sudden grief can be distressing. The whole body can go into shock: there can be shaking, fainting, nausea – everything collapses.

There are often 'unnatural' aspects to such deaths – accidents, suicide and murder can evoke feelings of blame and bitterness, disfigurement causes extra pain and some circumstances can cause us to have great feelings of (sometimes justified) guilt. The dead person may have left their affairs in disarray and there may be some nasty surprises.

Although, usually, grief will resolve itself in due course, sudden grief of this sort may need special attention, and yet these are the very situations where we can be reticent about giving support.

We can usually overcome our difficulties with bereavement when the death has been 'normal' but it's harder to approach the young widow whose husband took his own life with no warning or the parents of a murdered three-year-old.

We should see reports of sudden death as a salutary warning that it may be our turn next. How would your family be affected if you were killed in an accident tomorrow morning?

It's possible to be too preoccupied about the imminence of death – it's extremely unlikely to happen out of the blue, but it's worth us keeping a part of the back of our minds alert to the possibility. I'm not, however, suggesting we go this far:

> *Whenever I prepare for a journey I prepare as though for death. Should I never return, all is in order.*
> Katherine Mansfield, *Journal*, 1927

Hospice care

> *A rather rare combination of spirituality and hard medicine.*
> Unattributed

Although it is true that, in the past, social attitudes to death were more open and civilised, we ought not to underestimate the misery of the death bed for most people and their families before effective health services.

The rapid development of medicine in the middle of the twentieth century should have brought improvements but hospitals have been run as institutions to cure the sick: death has been 'the enemy'. Few hospital resources have been applied to those beyond further medical help and dying patients have been given little special care – only they are now isolated from the comfort of their families.

The key figure in the hospice movement is Dame Cecily Saunders. She was the person who not only established St Christopher's Hospice in London in 1967, but, more importantly, was able to articulate a campaign that has seen the expansion we know today.

In 1965 there were 15 hospices: now there are 228 in-patient hospices (with 3,307 beds), 245 day-care establishments, 478 home and community teams and 350 hospital support and palliative care services. There are 13 hospices specifically for children with a total of 106 beds.

Dr Saunders, for the first time, extended the function of the hospice from being a spiritually motivated institution where residents were kept simply and as comfortable as possible. She developed it to become the community provision we know today – actively involved with people with severe chronic disease and their families. As a doctor, she also pioneered medical advances in pain control.

The principles behind the hospice movement are to focus on caring for the whole person rather than a single disease. Therefore, for people near the end of their lives, it is important that medical care goes to the relief of symptoms, as well as giving attention to their other physiological, emotional, spiritual and family needs.

Conventional medical treatment is mainly concerned with a particular disease and will often be withdrawn if nothing further can be done. Doctors and nurses in hospices, however, will look more to the patient's feelings, hopes, fears and anxieties; they will know the importance of giving them – and their families – time and attention. They will also place a crucial value on honesty, openness and alertness to the patient's need to talk. However, there will be no wish to impose information, treatments or advice where they are not wanted.

People do die there but others are admitted and go home. There is no pattern laid down for someone's stay: people may come only for day care or may go in to give their carers some respite from heavy physical and emotional demands.

The aim is for dying people to be allowed to remain 'as much like themselves as possible': treatments aim for pain relief without any dulling of the senses in as positive and warm an environment as possible.

A doctor usually makes referrals but family members, friends or other health professionals can equally seek help.

The average hospice patient will have a life expectancy of six months or less.

The difference between a hospice and a hospital ward is very evident. They are more comfortably and generously furnished – people are encouraged to bring in important possessions. There are more staff with more time to spend with individuals and there is less emphasis on high-tech bed-care. There are no 'visiting hours' and the atmosphere will be welcoming and informal.

The cost of providing hospice care is usually less than a stay in hospital: there is usually less need for expensive diagnostic and therapeutic equipment and there is much more flexibility about admission and discharge home.

Hospice care is free of charge to patients and their families regardless of who provides it. The cost is funded by a combination of public donations, fund-raising activities and contracts between health authorities and hospice and specialist palliative care providers. As far as voluntary hospices are concerned, the NHS meets, on average, about 34 per cent of the costs of the services they provide.

Although it's true that many hospices may have a religious foundation, patients and staff are from any faith or none. Hospice and palliative care tries to meet the needs of people from all cultures and religions and those with no faith at all. If they are able, patients will be out of bed and as occupied inside or outside as much as they wish.

Because most hospices are set up by voluntary organisations, the distribution is patchy throughout the country: the number of places is limited – only about 7 per cent of people receive some sort of hospice care in the year before their death. There are only 3–4 per cent of the population who die in a hospice. Nevertheless, the hospice movement, small though it is, has been the engine behind greater public discussion about death. Its promise of pain-free, positive death has helped bring the subject out of the closet.

Today there are an increasing number of hospices being set up by secular organisations. We must not, however, imagine that those run by religious charities are solemn, prayerful places – they are most likely to be places filled with warmth and realism.

Each year there are 60,000 admissions, 30,000 deaths and 30,000 discharges from hospices.

More information can be obtained from:

◆ Hospice Information Service, St Christopher's Hospice, 51–59 Lawrie Park Road, Sydenham SE26 6DZ. Tel. (020) 8778 9252. Fax: (020) 8776 9345. Email. his@stchris.ftech.co.uk

This service can provide facts and figures about hospice provision in Britain and abroad for professionals and the public. Send £2.00 for a sample information pack. You should also be able to find out about local services from Citizens' Advice Bureaux or social services departments.

A hospice at home

There are a number of other organisations that provide an alternative to hospice care that will suit some people.

The NHS provides over 350 terminal care and support teams, based in hospitals, which aim to provide hospice-style services for people in hospital or who wish to remain at home. These can be brought in through your GP. The team is usually made up of a doctor, a nurse and a social worker. They work closely with other voluntary organisations to provide pain relief, advice, counselling, family support and practical help with home nursing and night sitting. Many people with terminal conditions wish to remain in their own familiar surroundings and their carers are all the more willing and able to continue if they can get some 'time off'.

The two principal voluntary nursing organisations are the Cancer Relief Macmillan Fund and Marie Curie Cancer Care who can be contacted locally through your doctor or district nurse.

Assisted death

> *No problem is insoluble given a big enough plastic bag.*
>
> Tom Stoppard

The muddle and ambivalence that we all have about the subject of dying is brought sharply into focus when we consider assisted death.

A favourite topic for radio phone-ins and debates, euthanasia – that's what it's usually called – can be relied on to stir strong feelings. It's a perfect topic for debate: it's an important subject, you can find as many people with strongly voiced opinions on either side and there's never a straightforward resolution.

Why is it that we can't sort out some system for dealing with it? Consider the following situation:

Case study: Margery _____

Margery is 57 years old, she is terminally ill with a condition which has brought about nearly total paralysis over the last eight years: she can do nothing for herself.

Her sight and hearing are failing. Her husband cared her for until he died three months ago: she has no children. Living alone, with a visiting home help and nurses, has increased her depression following her bereavement.

She is beginning to experience the slurring of speech and mental deterioration that she knows – as an ex-nurse – is the sign that the final stage of her illness is approaching.

She is a sensible, worldly and mature woman. Several times during the last couple of years she has raised the question of the possibility of assisted death with her GP: not now – but at that stage in the near future when she 'finally loses' her mind and becomes incapable of rational living.

Her fear is that she will lose the capacity to enjoy life and will need to be taken into a residential home or hospital. Her personal self-control and dignity are also important to her. She knows that she might well linger on in a state of complete and confused incapacity for many years.

Her GP and hospital consultant are both satisfied that her request for assistance with dying is long standing – entirely her own idea and well considered. Although she is depressed, she is not psychiatrically ill.

_____

Who could deny her this last great decision? Yet anyone who

helps her in her dying risks a charge of murder or assisting her suicide and could go to prison for many years. Another situation:

Case study: Steven _____

Steven has been in hospital for seven months. He had been in a severe motor vehicle crash, which had caused him to lose the use of his legs and blinded him in one eye.

He had been an active young man and was due to get married. Now it seemed the bottom had fallen out of his world. His fiancée had left him. He was in a specialist spinal unit 150 miles from home, which meant that he rarely had visitors.

He did nothing, read nothing, watched no TV: his grumpiness did not go down with the nurses and other patients. He could see nothing in the future and just wanted 'a pill to end it all'. _____

It is inconceivable that the law should allow a responsible doctor to assist Steven's death. So many possibilities had not been explored: psychotherapy; physio and occupational therapy; a move nearer home; retraining; independent living accommodation . . . .

These two examples illustrate the difficulty of the present situation: Margery is denied her dignified death because we are afraid that any new regulations would allow Steven also to be assisted to die. (See Appendix 1 for some insight into current public opinion about assisted death.)

The lack of clarity and agreed practice about what goes on at the moment makes it possible that, unguided, Steven's doctor may well feel justified in making a lonely, secret – and wrong – decision to help him out of misplaced human compassion.

It is unfortunate that assisted death should be debated as being 'right' or 'wrong': it is very complex and there are many elements. We're talking about:

♦ people who have been unconscious for years
♦ people who would commit suicide tomorrow if they could manage it
♦ people who are psychiatrically disordered
♦ people who 'don't want to be a burden'
♦ people who don't want their life savings eaten up with years

of residential care costs

- pressures from relatives
- fears of patients, relatives and doctors
- a patient's right to autonomy
- medical paternalism
- murder, manslaughter and the criminal law
- availability of resources
- quality of hospital and hospice care
- questions about who makes the decision
- questions about safeguards.

If we then take into account the variations of knowledge, maturity, care and commitment of all the potential participants, together with the difficulties involved in making accurate assessments of people's intentions and understanding, it becomes clear that it is probably not possible to frame legislation which satisfies everybody and answers all objections.

The trouble is that to do nothing is even more unsatisfactory. As potential patients requiring future assistance, we'll see later what we can do about this sad state of affairs.

Assisted deaths are increasing

We're all living longer. The older we get the more we're likely to suffer long, debilitating terminal diseases such as Alzheimer's disease (one person in four over 85 years will have this condition):

- Technological advances mean that more and more, unconscious lives can be sustained longer. At any one time in Britain (1999) there are 1,000 people who have been in a persistent vegetative state for more than six months.
- Because of our sophistication in life sustenance, it is becoming increasingly more difficult to define death.
- We're becoming more and more aware of our right for our voices to be heard.
- We no longer have such easy access to methods of suicide – especially if we are disabled. Drugs are much safer and less accessible. Even our cookers are supplied with 'the wrong sort of gas'.

◆ We have a much more relaxed relationship with our
doctors: they have lost much of their mystique and we feel
better able to ask questions and challenge decisions.

The British law about assisted death

There isn't one. To assist someone to die is to commit a crime.
The same law that deals with murder applies – the Homicide
Act 1957.

A charge of murder can be made if there is an intention to
shorten someone's life even by a few hours or minutes. The
prosecution has to prove that it was the drug – and not the
illness – which caused the death, though even if they can't,
there can still be a finding of attempted murder. In practice,
however, where there is a prosecution, it is for manslaughter.

Prosecutions have been few and a reduction of the charge to
manslaughter means that the sentence can be less and does not
necessarily involve imprisonment.

Nevertheless, to ask your doctor to assist your dying is to
invite her potentially to have to own up to either murder or
substantially impaired mental responsibility: there's also a
permanent criminal record and possible professional damage.

Although since 1961 it has not been a crime to take, or
attempt to take, your own life, it is an offence under the
Suicide Act 1961 for someone to help you. There have been
only a few prosecutions resulting usually in a suspended
sentence or probation – but there have been some custodial
sentences. Maybe the tacit uncertainty is appropriate and keeps
everyone on their toes.

> *Voltaire famously reported that in this country we like to*
> *execute an admiral occasionally 'pour encourager les autres'.*
> *On the same basis, it is probably a good thing to prosecute the*
> *occasional doctor.*
>
> Richard Ingrams, *Observer*, 6 May 1999

In spite of the uncertainties and threat of prosecution, there is
no doubt that we are generally in favour of assisted dying in
certain circumstances – and doctors are actually doing it. In a
survey in the magazine *Doctor* (February 1995), 79 per cent of

respondents (doctors) said that assisted death was 'an accepted part of medical practice'.

A *British Medical Journal* survey in 1996 showed that 60 per cent of doctors had been asked by patients for help with dying and 32 per cent of these doctors had agreed to do so. This means that one doctor in five has helped someone die and technically is an unconvicted criminal.

Elsewhere in the *BMJ* survey, 46 per cent of the doctors wanted to see assisted death legalised but only 37 per cent would actually be willing to carry it out. When it comes to withholding or withdrawing treatment in order to hasten a patient's death, a massive 92 per cent agreed they would do that 'in certain circumstances'.

There is less support for a more liberal law from religious groups, most of which have strong feelings about the sanctity of life or the significance of a 'natural' death.

More white, disabled or English people are in favour of change than people from other ethnic groups, people without a disability or those from Scotland.

There is interest in the subject wherever you look – except for Parliament. A survey in *The House* in 1997 showed that only 27 per cent of MPs supported assisted death in principle. One suggested reason for this is that the subject is so complex and raises so many feelings that it isn't amenable to effective public discussion without alienating large numbers of voters.

So, it's forbidden by law, in all circumstances, to help us to die or even to advise us how we might go about it ourselves.

In this way a conspiracy of uncertainty and secrecy has been established which is in the interests of neither those who are 'for' nor those who are 'against' assisted death.

The Netherlands

The difficulty of writing an all-encompassing law has been partially overcome in The Netherlands. It is still illegal to assist someone to die but for the last 18 years it has been established public policy that if a doctor follows a prescribed procedure, no action will be taken.

The conditions are that the patient has made repeated requests for help and that their suffering should be assessed as unrelievable and unacceptable. The doctor should seek other medical opinions to confirm his assessment and the circumstances should be recorded and reported to the local medical examiner.

This works well because The Netherlands has a reputation for high quality social and medical care of older and disabled people: resources are available for options other than assisted death – all hospitals, for example, have palliative care services.

The whole process is open and publicly acknowledged: it's called 'a medical decision to end life' – no bones about it. What is so unsavoury about all sides to the discussion in Britain is the unspoken secrecy: the nods and winks. When it's illegal it can't be discussed, regulated or monitored.

A survey in early 1999, however, reveals that things may not be quite so rosy. It seems that about one in five terminations may have been done without proper consent. In addition, in the same proportion of cases, it was not performed as a last resort – but as an alternative to palliative care.

In The Netherlands about 4,000 people die every year with the help of their doctor (although the unofficial estimate is about 26,000): if this figure of 4,000 was reflected in the British population it would be 20,000 people. There is legislation planned for 2001, which will allow assisted death and suicide to be fully acceptable and legal.

(The Netherlands has strict rules which prevent non-Dutch people from taking advantage of regulations for assisted dying.)

If I can choose between a death of torture and one that is simple and easy, why should I not select the latter? As I choose the ship in which I sail and the house which I inhabit, so will I choose the death by which I leave life.

Seneca

What if someone asks for our help?

Providing information and supplying the means may be the basis for a criminal prosecution in the United Kingdom although the law has not been effectively tested. For this reason, and in order to act with integrity, it is most important that we act carefully and give thought to our responsibilities:

unfortunately the decision falls to us alone about whether our involvement is not only 'proper' but can also be later explained to have been correct.

We must be confident that we have a close, loving and respectful relationship with the person involved. A casual acquaintance or estranged spouse is not someone who should have anything to do with an assisted death.

We must (arrogantly – we've no choice) be sure in our mind that the person is acting rationally and is not being unduly influenced by treatable depression or pressure from others.

It's important to give no physical assistance in administering drugs or other means of assisted death.

Make sure that the dying person has set out their wishes and intentions in writing – it may be necessary later to establish what happened and why.

Involuntary assisted death

So far we've been looking at issues surrounding voluntary assisted death – where you're in a position to explain your wishes. What would you like to happen to you if you were not in a position to give or withhold consent – when it is also not very clear whether you are 'alive' or not?

These are situations where you might be in a coma – or a persistent vegetative state (PVS). This is when the brain stem is alive and the patient is able to breathe for himself, but the cerebral cortex (the thinking, feeling and communicating part of the brain) is irreparably damaged.

A persistent vegetative state arises from an injury to the brain following a lack of oxygen, sugar deprivation or some other event. This causes the patient to fall into a coma. Younger people have more chance of recovery: older people or people whose condition was caused by oxygen starvation (the usual cause) are less likely to recover.

After six months (a year for children) recovery is very rare indeed. At this point they are declared to be in a 'permanent vegetative state'. The PVS patient cannot feel pain, is fed by tubes implanted in the stomach and is unable to communicate.

Often artificial feeding and nursing care are sufficient to

keep the patient alive indefinitely – decades even. As it becomes clear that recovery is unlikely, the question will arise about stopping feeding and allowing them to die.

Most doctors (92 per cent) in a *BMJ* survey in 1996 believed there were circumstances where the withholding or withdrawal of treatment in order to hasten a patient's death could be justified. Seven out of ten believed it acceptable to withdraw artificial nutrition and hydration (ANH) and this figure rose to eight out of ten where the patient had been in PVS for at least 12 months.

For many years doctors had acted in the dark with no firm guidelines. Then in 1993 the parents of Tony Bland, who had been in PVS for several years, were given permission from the High Court to halt artificial feeding. These set a precedent and since then about a dozen other cases have come to court and permissions granted.

Then in 1996, news came of two patients who had been in PVS for seven years at the Royal Hospital for Neuro-disability in Putney: they had regained some consciousness and begun to communicate. However, they remain severely brain-damaged, immobile and tube fed. Their doctor, Dr Keith Andrews, claimed that 17 out of 40 patients, said to be in PVS, had been misdiagnosed and might recover.

Many families have new hope with stories like these; they wish to keep relatives alive hoping a miracle will happen – there is one PVS patient in America who has survived 43 years.

However, there is no evidence that patients who have been in PVS for years (rather than months), even when they do recover, have what most people would consider an acceptable quality of life.

Although formal standards and procedures have so far only been accepted for patients in persistent vegetative states, there is growing concern among doctors that there need to be rules for patients with other conditions – for example, people with profound Alzheimer's disease, severely brain-damaged babies and victims of severe strokes.

Brain-stem death

This is, perhaps, the most straightforward assisted death to deal with. In this case, not only has the patient been unconscious for a length of time and is being fed artificially, but the brain stem has ceased to work and is no longer able to sustain the basic ability of the body to remain alive. Life is continuing only thanks to a respirator and other technical equipment.

There is thought to be no chance that the patient will recover. The problem is that often the person gives all the outward appearance of being in good health – their chest is moving, their colour is good: they look as though they are asleep. It seems wrong somehow to suggest that the respirator should be switched off – meaning certain and immediate death.

It is, however, possible to carry out a series of carefully detailed tests to confirm brain-stem death. (This is different from someone in PVS whose brain stem is alive and controlling vital functions – they are suffering from other brain damage from which they may or may not recover.)

The brain-stem test

After testing that the patient's condition is not related to any medication or underlying medical cause (such as anti-depressants, hypothermia, drug intoxication), there is a series of established tests to check irremediable brain-stem death; the results will be confirmed by repeating them after a period of hours. There should be:

♦ no spontaneous body movements
♦ no response to painful stimuli, e.g. pinpricks or pressure on the fingernail
♦ inability to breathe without a ventilator; no respiratory reflex
♦ irremediable structural brain damage
♦ fixated, dilated pupils giving no response to light
♦ no reflexes of the cornea
♦ no response to extreme cold
♦ no vomit reflex.

It's important to emphasise that where all these tests were stringently carried out and there were negative results, no PVS patient has *ever* recovered consciousness.

What have you got to say to your family in your advance

directive about what should happen to you in these circumstances? I'm sure they would like to know.

Willed fasting

When terminally ill people are beyond the help of medical therapies we assume that at least we can keep them comfortable: we encourage them to keep up their nutrition and fluid intake – at least we can prevent hunger and thirst.

There have been recent studies, however, which indicate that when the body is in ultimate decline the need for food and liquid drops markedly.

Our lifelong experience is that taking in an adequate amount of the right kind of food and lots of liquid is our first priority: we consider the effect of food and liquid deprivation as cruel, inhuman and life-threatening.

A fit 40-year-old person can fast for about six weeks before there is a serious threat to life. After you lose about 20 per cent of your normal body weight, deterioration sets in: indigestion, muscle weakness or mental deterioration. To be forcibly starved is usually torture.

The dying body, however, seems to recognise the futility of feeding and nourishing dying tissue: the agonies of hunger and thirst that a healthy person would suffer – especially from lack of liquid – seem to diminish.

Often dying people will not be inclined to eat and drink but will continue for fear of the hunger and thirst to be expected: this will be encouraged by those around them. However, real loss of appetite and absence of thirst may be nature's way of enabling a speedy release from extended suffering. Often the wish to drink is simply to relieve a dryness in the mouth.

A study quoted in *Beyond Final Exit* published by the Right to Die Association of Canada came to some surprising conclusions:

◆ There was widespread support amongst hospice workers for allowing dehydration in some terminal patients.
◆ 53 per cent of nurses agreed that dehydration can be beneficial for the dying.
◆ 71 per cent agreed that dehydration reduces the incidence of vomiting.

- 73 per cent agreed that dehydrated patients rarely complain of thirst: a dry mouth can be helped with sips of water or chips of ice.
- 51 per cent reported that choking and drowning sensations were reduced when fluids are discontinued.
- Dehydration was not painful in these patients and made for a more comfortable death.

No one is suggesting that terminally ill patients should be 'encouraged' to fast: many people will wish to continue to eat and drink as before. Clearly much more research is needed. However, this research indicates that where someone clearly does not wish to eat or drink, then there may be good reason for this and their body may be wiser than we may know.

Crypthanasia

This is the rather lurid description of the act of assisting someone's death in their interests but without their knowledge. Can you think of any circumstances when this would be justified?

I suppose it would need to be a situation where you had knowledge that something catastrophic, involving much suffering, was certain to happen to someone and it would definitely result in their death. You should also have the means to cause the death as quickly and painlessly as possible. There have been instances during wartime when someone's capture, torture and death were certain and someone with the knowledge and the means was able to 'slip them something' to avoid distress and suffering.

But I can't see anything like that would happen here in the West Midlands.

*I feel nothing
except a certain
difficulty in
continuing to
exist.*

BERNARD DE
FONTANELLE

CHAPTER 4

The Day Itself Has Arrived

A ll deaths are, of course, different from each other. It
would be comforting to believe that there is nothing to
be feared in the process. For many people, even if the worst of
the pain is relieved, there is nausea, confusion or mental
distress: for others there will be drug-induced oblivion.

However, commonly, the experience is less dramatic.

The physical process of dying

Most people who have been able to prepare for the end openly
with their loved ones and who are receiving good pain relief
and support will, surprisingly perhaps, be in a state of quiet
acceptance.

This calmness is not 'brave' or psychologically induced.
When the body is in its ultimate crisis we are provided with
our own internally manufactured supply of endorphins. This is
a final first-aid support from the brain, which senses that all
may be over and the best, last, survival hope is to stay calm, do
nothing and to resist panic. It is the same process that protects
us in severe accidents – the pain and distress are temporarily
anaesthetised. Perhaps this is the answer to Max Frisch's
(*Sketchbook* 1966–71) question:

Why do dying people never shed tears?

When we die our life is not extinguished as with a light switch.
It is a process during which our body systems gradually close
down: we fade into death.

Our first awareness that the end is near is that the senses
begin to lose definition. We may be able to hear people talking
but the individual words become unclear. We will notice that
the detail fades from what we can see: and so with the other
senses.

The strength and energy begin to drain from our body: we

can't sit up or grip things; our head needs support. There is a sensation of falling and heaviness in our limbs. We may be uncomfortably sensitive to the weight of the bed covers.

The blood drains from our face and our cheeks sink inwards. Opening and closing the eyes becomes difficult. We feel weak and frail, our thoughts become erratic and confused and then drowsiness sets in.

We relax control over bodily fluids. The nose runs, we dribble saliva, our eyes moisten and we may pass urine. The fine muscles in our tongue won't respond. Our eyes and mouth feel dry and congested and our nostrils begin to collapse. There may be some muscular twitching.

The thought processes begin to disintegrate alternating between clarity and vagueness. We can feel our body heat draining away, from the hands and feet at first.

Our shallower breathing is cold against the inside of the mouth and nose. Breathing in is harder, breathing out is slower. All sensations become blurred as unconsciousness begins to take over.

As worldly and physical awareness fades there are inner sensations of lightness, release and floating. This is the near-death experience (described elsewhere) which *may* be caused by complex chemical changes in the senses and the brain, but which on the whole remains unexplained.

Then there is the moment when the heart stops which we call the 'time of death': we become irreversibly unconscious and lose all awareness of the world and ourselves: the muscles relax completely.

However, although this is usually the point of no return, different parts of the body will remain alive for some minutes more or longer. Cells in the brain, for example, will remain alive for three to seven minutes.

It is not unusual, shortly after the time of death, for the contents of the stomach to be regurgitated into the throat and for urine and semen to be emitted.

The first sure sign to those present that death has occurred will be a sharp drop in body temperature – *algor mortis*. Dependent on the temperature of the room and the body mass of the individual, this can be completed in a short time or up to twelve hours on the skin. The body temperature will rise again after a couple of days because of the metabolic action of bacteria and other decomposition processes.

Within minutes of death it will be clear from the lifeless face that this is different from unconsciousness: the skin takes on a grey-white pallor and the appearance is clearly corpse-like.

The eyes confirm death. Within four or five minutes the twinkle goes, they become dull and the pupils dilate: the cornea in the eye films over and the white becomes grey. The eyeballs flatten, the cornea clouds after a couple of hours and becomes opaque after a day or two. (After about three days there is a build-up of gas in the eyes, which causes them to bulge: this bulging reduces after further decomposition.)

The pulse has stopped and the skin loses elasticity and 'life'. The central nervous system dies first but other parts of the body, less crucially dependent on immediate oxygen, can take a little longer.

Normally blood is evenly distributed throughout the body. When it is no longer being circulated it sinks by gravity making the areas where it settles dark blue or purple – like bruising. This begins immediately and is visible after a couple of hours. After five or six hours this settlement is complete.

Some muscles may respond to electrical stimulation hours after death: skin and bone cells can live for several days and, if there were any point, liver cells would still be able to function for a few hours. The rate at which cells die depends on their ability to continue without oxygen and to tolerate a build-up of waste products. Richard Seizer described these last signs of life as:

> *outposts where clusters of cells yet shine, besieged, little lights blinking in the advancing darkness. Doomed soldiers, they battle on. Until Death has secured the premises all to itself.*
>
> Mortal Lessons, 1987

There is no single point when death can be said to have happened. Rather, (vaguely) it is that stage in the process of dying when the person seems to lack:

> *The features that humans must possess to be regarded as living persons rather than dead persons.*
>
> R. G. Gervaise, *Redefining Death*, Yale University Press, 1987

Because muscle cells are no longer being fed, lactic acid is produced. This forms a complex reaction in the muscle tissue that results in the characteristic stiffness of *rigor mortis*. If there are high levels of lactic acid already in the muscles – if, for example, death took place during heavy exercise – the onset of *rigor mortis* will develop relatively quickly. The chemical process will also be speeded up in a high environmental temperature.

The rate of stiffening can also be affected by particular illnesses. Normally, however, at room temperature, *rigor mortis* will begin to set in after one to four hours in the small muscles of the face and hands and after about two to six hours in the larger muscles: this will depend on the age, sex, physical condition and muscular build of the individual. It will be complete after about 24 hours and can last 36–48 hours. It will first affect the eyelids and face and then move down the rest of the body. The rigidity will then relax into a gradual state of flaccidity.

The one fact that we thought we knew – that hair and nails continue to grow after death – is untrue: the impression of growth is caused by the follicles at the base of the hairs becoming stiffened and making them stick out, giving the effect of increased fullness.

Changes in body temperature and flaccidity after death

Warm and limp	Up to 3 hours after death
Warm and stiff	3–8 hours after death
Cold and stiff	8–36 hours after death
Cold and limp	Dead more than 36 hours

Putrefaction of body tissue begins after about two days. This is usually arrested by refrigeration. Given this precaution there will not be the odour, decaying, blistering and discoloration we might fear. Very hot, dry air temperatures also prevent it – the body will dry out and become mummified.

Within the intestine, particularly the colon, we are all hosts to many types of internal organisms and bacteria – microbes make up 90 per cent of all the cells in the body (by number). (Fifty per cent of faecal material is made up of bacteria). In life these are kept in check and play an important part in digestion. After death, however, our bodies are unprotected by our immune system and, not believing their luck, a host of microbes begin to multiply rapidly and set off to invade previously prohibited body territory.

Apart from bacterial activity the bodily tissues themselves undergo decomposition because of the release of enzymes and other chemicals: the enzymes produced in life to digest food now begin to consume the digestive system itself.

The first sign of this activity will be a greenish discoloration of the skin on the chest, lower abdomen and upper thighs: there will also be a putrid odour. This colouring and smell is caused by sulphur-saturated gas produced from bacterial action and the chemical breakdown of red blood cells.

The gas production will saturate the intestine walls, blood vessels and other tissues that will break down, spreading the decomposition to other organs.

Four to six days after death, at normal room temperature, the whole body can become bloated with the gas pressure if it is not released (often an incision is made into the abdomen). If this happens the tongue and eyes may protrude, the intestines may be forced into the rectum and vagina and the skin may change colour from green to purple and black. The pressure may cause bloodstained fluid to exude from the nose, mouth and other orifices.

This putrefaction can be successfully kept in check by refrigeration or embalming and it can be suspended by freezing. It can also be accelerated if the cause of death was an overwhelming bacterial infection.

After the decomposition process is complete the body loses all semblance of previous life but during the process of change there is a transitional stage where evidence of the living person persists. Jonathan Miller recollects his days as a medical student:

When I went into the post-mortem room they were recently dead; they had that faint candle-wax, sort of tallow appearance and they were flexible – and that was disturbing because they had been human beings very recently and there was that warm butcher's smell, a mixture of a butcher's and a lavatory. It was a smell of newly opened gut, a smell of warm farts.

They were still very near to human beings but unrecognisable, in the sense that you couldn't see them as someone you might recognise in the street. They were recognisably people because they had this sort of... they looked like someone that you might say to 'You look ill': that sort of awful yellow greenness.

Quoted in *The Ruffian on the Stair* by
Rosemary Dinnage, Viking 1990

After about a week (again, unrefrigerated), most of the body surface becomes discoloured and there will be large, putrid blistering of the skin – causing the top layer to come away under pressure.

The rate of decomposition will be reduced if the body is enclosed and protected from insect invasion. The 'worms' that we associate with decomposition are not the familiar earthworms we see in the garden but maggots produced from flies; beetles, moths and mites will also join in.

After another week the breasts, abdomen, tongue and scrotum swell. Three or four weeks after death the hair, nails and teeth loosen and the internal organs will rupture and liquefy.

If the body has been buried, the coffin is likely to disintegrate after a few weeks and the increased moisture will hasten the decay. Tough ligaments will resist a little longer as, strangely, will the prostate gland and the uterus.

Eventually the cells in all the tissues of the body will gradually become disorganised. Their various chemical structures and components will break down and dissolve into a soup, if the body is not kept chilled.

Between them, bacteria, insects and natural breakdown of tissues will reduce a body to a skeleton in a year or two. Depending on the acidity, temperature, moisture and shallowness of the soil, bones will dissolve in from 25 to 100 years in temperate climates. However, in cool, dry environments our reduction to dust could take 200–500 years. Carbon, nitrogen and phosphorus are released from the 'dust' and recycled within the soil to feed growth above. We eat the plants... and so on....

In exceptional circumstances (ancient Egypt, for example)

where internal organs were removed and the body tissues dried out before they could be attacked by internal decomposition or external infestation, bodies became mummified.

This destructive process of decomposition is described by Richard Selzer, an American writer, in his book *Mortal Lessons* – surprisingly poetically:

> *There is to be a feast. The rich table has been set. The board groans. The guests have already arrived, numberless bacteria that had in life, dwelt in saprophytic harmony with their host. Their turn now!*
>
> *Charged, they press against the membrane barriers, break through the new softness, sweep across plains of tissue. Devouring, belching gas – a gas that puffs eyelids, cheeks, abdomen into bladders of murderous vapor. The slimmest man takes on the bloat of corpulence. Your swollen belly bursts with a ripping sound, followed by a long mean hiss.*
>
> *And they are large! Blisters appear upon the skin, enlarge, coalesce, blast, leaving brownish puddles in the declivities. You are becoming gravy... Gray sprays of fungus sprout in the resulting marinade, and there lacks only a mushroom growing from the nose.*

Laying-out and preparing a body

Laying-out happens once the doctor has certified the cause of death and when it is clear that the coroner is not going to be involved. The body must not be moved before the doctor has been.

Anyone can do the laying-out: it requires no special skill or knowledge (see Appendix II for details). However, it may well be that, because of the unfortunate squeamishness we have in the face of the reality of death, some people do not feel able to do it. It's a highly individual decision: one spouse might see it as an important last act of care: another, overcome with feelings of loss, may not be able to face such an intimate confrontation with the physical reality of death. Usually it will be dealt with by a funeral director.

There is no 'need' for a body to be laid out – many people consider it disrespectful to the dead person. However, after some deaths, when there has been an unusual build up of gas inside the body, if all the orifices are sealed the whole body may become bloated and an incision may need to be made to release the pressure. So long as the body is kept chilled and is lying on a waterproof sheet to collect any leakage, laying-out is often unnecessary.

A funeral director has a special cold room for storage. If the body is kept at home, use an unheated room with open windows. If the weather is hot it might be worth hiring a portable air-conditioning unit to keep the temperature down: an alternative is to use dry ice packed around the abdomen.

Some people have rigged up a sealed 'tent' around an open refrigerator. (Of course, it's no good at all just to have an open refrigerator in the room.)

There are special rules for deaths from certain 'notifiable diseases':

◆ cholera
◆ smallpox
◆ plague
◆ typhus
◆ AIDS
◆ relapsing fever.

According to public health legislation, a magistrate can direct immediate burial or cremation of the body (or removal to a mortuary) if the place where it is being kept is likely to cause a risk to public health. There must be no unnecessary contact with the body.

Registering the death

Since 1837 it has been compulsory to register the fact and cause of every death. Not only does this provide a check on any suspicious circumstances, but it is a useful way of gathering important statistics about public health.

Normally the GP will have examined the body recently and will be able to write out a Cause of Death Certificate, which should be taken in person to the Registrar for the death to be registered. In exceptional circumstances – maybe if you're disabled – the Registrar will come to your home to register the death.

However, although the next of kin may feel responsible for doing it, any relative can register the details who was:

◆ present at the death, *or*
◆ was present during the last illness, *or*
◆ is resident in the area where the death occurred.

Certain other people who can give direct evidence of the death are also eligible to register the death.

All deaths should be registered within five days in England, Wales and Northern Ireland. There are two purposes for registration:

◆ to confirm the identity of the deceased
◆ to establish the cause of death.

The body can be released for burial or cremation only when the Registrar is satisfied about the person's identity and the cause of death.

In most cases, this will be straightforward. As well as the Cause of Death Certificate, the informant needs to take:

◆ birth and marriage certificates
◆ the deceased's medical card
◆ any state benefits books.

They will also want to know:

◆ the full name of the deceased (and maiden name if applicable)
◆ any other names the deceased was known by
◆ date and place of birth
◆ date and place of death
◆ last address
◆ occupation
◆ name, date of birth and occupation of spouse (or previous spouse)
◆ whether the deceased was receiving any state benefits.

The Registrar will then issue a Certificate for Burial (also known as the Green Forrn). This must be given to anyone organising arrangements before the funeral can take place.

If cremation is preferred, your doctor needs to complete a form as well as a second independent doctor. Both doctors must certify the cause of death and that no further examination of the body is necessary. This was originally intended as a safeguard in response to the accusation in the nineteenth century that cremation was an ideal way to dispose of murder victims.

Your first costs are incurred here because each doctor will charge £41.00 to complete the form. Normally a funeral director will include these charges in his bill.

With so much paperwork and so many certificates, the death certificate – which is the only one we had heard about beforehand – is the least important. It is not a legal requirement for it to be issued, but the next of kin will find it useful as evidence of death in settling the deceased's affairs or essential should they wish to remarry in the future. It is simply a copy of the entry in the Register and you will have to pay £3.50 for it (more if you need a copy later). You can have more than one copy. Otherwise, there are no other charges in registering a death.

It's worth contacting the Registrar before you go to register the death to make an appointment so that you don't have to sit about. The telephone number will be listed under 'Registrar of Births, Deaths and Marriages'.

It is also advisable for the informant, who is likely to be in some distress faced with all these formalities, to take someone along for support.

Complications

There will be times when this complex business of registration seems to be made even more difficult. It is important, however, to realise that all these procedures are necessary as public safeguards of the deceased's interests. They are not intended to be officious and bureaucratic and will be handled sensitively.

Nevertheless, emotionally vulnerable relatives may well be forgiven if they feel obstructed, disbelieved or under suspicion when all they want to do is complete the formalities quickly and put things to rest.

If a doctor has not examined the deceased within the last

14 days (in England and Wales) (28 days in Northern Ireland), the Coroner (Procurator Fiscal in Scotland) must be informed. In Scotland, there is no time limit but the doctor has to be convinced that the cause was natural.

The Coroner has to be informed of all sudden deaths before a Certificate of Cause of Death can be issued. She also needs to be told:

◆ where death has been caused as a result of an industrial disease, accident, violence, neglect, poisoning or abortion
◆ where it has happened in police or prison custody
◆ where medical or surgical treatment was taking place in hospital.

About 15 per cent of all deaths are reported to the Coroner.

Where the GP can assure the Coroner that the cause is natural and evident – even though he hasn't visited within the time limit – the Coroner can agree to issue a Cause of Death Certificate. Funeral arrangements can then proceed as normal.

The fact that a doctor refuses to give an immediate Cause of Death Certificate and has to refer the death to the Coroner is no cause for suspicion or anxiety (he has no option).

It is also routine for the police to wish to take statements where there is a sudden death. Although this can be felt as intrusive and unnecessary, it is an important formality and safeguard. This will involve the police arranging for a formal identification of the body.

If the cause of death cannot be immediately determined, a post-mortem will have to be carried out as quickly as possible by a pathologist. There is no choice in this: by law, a post-mortem must take place in uncertain circumstances, even if it is distressing to the bereaved – even, sadly, if it is in against the religious beliefs of some people (although it can be contested in the High Court – taking time and expense).

If the next of kin wishes, they can arrange for an independent pathologist to repeat the post-mortem on their behalf. If the pathologist can report that the death was a natural one, the Coroner or Procurator Fiscal will issue a Cause of Death Certificate, which will usually be sent directly to the Registrar.

However, often things are not so clear and there needs to be a further investigation. In such circumstances the Coroner or

Procurator Fiscal can order a fatal accident enquiry or inquest. Usually this happens when:

◆ there is still uncertainty about the cause of death
◆ there may have been a crime involved
◆ there is a suspicion of suicide
◆ the body has not been found (following a drowning, for example)
◆ there may be an insurance claim or a claim for compensation following an accidental death, an industrial injury, a death during medical treatment or a death in custody.

The purpose of an inquest is to establish how the person died and what happened to cause it. It is not the job of the Coroner to decide who is to blame – although the police or some other authority may well act on this separately.

Family members can attend the inquest and, with the consent of the Coroner, they can ask witnesses questions (or use a solicitor – although no legal aid is available). It is important, if there is any question of a subsequent claim for damages or compensation, that you are legally represented. When the evidence has been considered – sometimes with the help of a jury – the Coroner will sum up and issue one of several verdicts. Examples of these could be:

◆ natural causes
◆ accidental death – a straightforward accident
◆ misadventure – an accident resulting from a deliberate act of the dead person
◆ suicide
◆ unlawful killing – murder or manslaughter
◆ an open verdict.

Sometimes, further time is needed for enquiries to proceed and the inquest can be adjourned; there may be a fuller enquiry continuing into an accident or the police may not have completed a criminal investigation.

If there is an adjournment and if the body is no longer required for examination, the Coroner will issue an Order for Cremation or Burial, which will enable the next of kin to get on with the important task of arranging the funeral and sorting out the estate.

Finally the Coroner will organise the registration of the death directly and the family can get copies of the death certificate in the usual way.

> See Appendix IV for a checklist of paperwork and other 'things to do' after a death.

Post-mortems

> *In the chest in the heart was the vessel*
> *was the pulse was the art was the love*
> *was the clot small and slow and the scar*
> *that could not know*
> *the rest of you*
> *was very nearly perfect.*
>
> John Stone, 'Autopsy in the Form of an Elegy',
> quoted in *Death To Dust*, Iserson

There are many reasons for and benefits of a post-mortem:

- ◆ Evidence can be gleaned where death has occurred in unexpected or suspicious circumstances.
- ◆ The grief process of bereaved relatives can be helped: fantasies about it being 'my fault' or 'if only another treatment had been tried...' can be assuaged: worries about inherited disease can often be put to rest.
- ◆ New diseases can be discovered, medical complications before death can be clarified, new technologies and procedures can be evaluated and medical students can be educated about the course of a disease.
- ◆ Public health can be protected by the identification of infectious or contagious disease. Occupational health and environmental hazards can be identified. Medical statistics can be obtained.
- ◆ Family health risks can be identified: genetic counselling can be recommended.
- ◆ Evidence can be obtained for insurance or litigation purposes.

What happens?

> *Above each of the slabs, there is a hanging scale such as is*

*used in delicatessen stores. Now and then, a kidney will flop
up on the scale, then bounce itself to stillness. 'Right
kidney... 200 grams,' a voice calls out. Somewhere this is
recorded. The kidney is retrieved from the scale; cubes and
slices of it are taken and arranged on trays. From these pieces,
microscopic slides will be made.*

Richard Selzer, *Confessions of a Knife*

The first stage in a post-mortem is to examine the outside of
the body for any unusual signs or blemishes: relevant X-rays
may be taken.

The chest is then opened with a cut centrally down the
body or a Y-shaped incision – beginning at each armpit,
joining beneath the breasts at the bottom of the breastbone and
moving down the centre of the abdomen to end at the pubis,
just above the genital area. The skin is turned back and the
whole of the front part of the rib cage is removed in one piece.
This exposes most of the internal organs, which can then be
examined for any abnormality of size or position, which might
have affected their functioning.

If it is relevant to the likely cause of death, the brain may
be examined. This is done by cutting the skin in a line from
ear to ear across the base of the scalp and peeling the front
part over the face and the back over the nape of the neck. The
skull is now fully exposed and the upper part is removed using
a high-speed surgical saw. The surface of the brain and the
inside surface of the 'skull cap' are then examined for any
injury or sign of disease.

In normal circumstances pathologists will try to leave the
skin on the face, neck and upper torso undisturbed.

Next the internal organs are removed from the chest for
examination:

*The following procedure is quite common: major vessels at the
base of the neck are tied and the oesophagus and trachea
(windpipe) are severed just above the thyroid cartilage
(Adam's apple). They pinch off the aorta above the diaphragm
and cut it along with the inferior vena cava, allowing the heart
and lungs to be removed together, but leaving the oesophagus
in place. The spleen is then separately removed from the*

abdomen, as are the small and large intestines. The liver,
pancreas, stomach and oesophagus are removed as a unit,
followed by the kidneys, ureters, bladder and abdominal aorta.
Finally the testes are removed. The pathologist then takes small
samples of muscle, nerve and fibrous tissue from the various
organs for microscopic examination. The spinal cord itself is
rarely removed. However, if it is to be examined, the backbone
is cut with a special saw and the cord is lifted out.

Kenneth Iserson, *From Death to Dust*, Galen Press

The organs are opened and their structures are examined for
abnormalities. If necessary, the brain is removed after severing
attachments to the spinal cord, skull, blood vessels and nerve
connections.

Bones are rarely removed but if they have to be they are
replaced with plastic, wooden or metal prostheses.

If a pacemaker has been fitted this is removed and sent
away for technical examination for any defects.

Throughout this whole procedure – which can last between
1 and 3 hours – every finding is described and recorded
meticulously and in a way that will commonly be understood
by future readers. The first part of the post-mortem is now
complete: the organs are replaced in the body cavity and all the
exterior incisions are sewn up.

The second stage of the post-mortem begins when relevant
tissue and fluid specimens are tested in the laboratory: this can
be time-consuming, as some tests do not give immediate
results. There will be routine tests for alcohol, drugs and other
chemical agents.

When all the results are available the pathologist will make
an assessment of the cause of death and the contributing
factors.

There was a study by D. A. Mosquera in 1993 (*Annals of the
Royal College of Surgeons*) which revealed that pathologists had
discovered that, at post-mortem, two-thirds of the subjects had
been misdiagnosed by their doctors and that, of these, a
quarter might have survived if there had been a correct
diagnosis.

In another more recent study, looking at post-mortems of
people over 80, pathologists were unable to find a particular
cause of death in a third of the subjects.

CHAPTER 5

Arranging a Funeral

And when they
buried him, the
little port
Had seldom
seen a costlier
funeral.
TENNYSON,
'ENOCH ARDEN',
1864

*A funeral is a pageant whereby we attest our respect for the
dead by enriching the undertaker and strengthen our grief
by an expenditure that deepens our groans and doubles our tears.*
Ambrose Bierce, A Devil's Dictionary

The funeral director

The funeral industry in Britain is a huge and controversial
business worth around £1 billion per year. About 4,000 funeral
directors arrange 640,000 funerals a year. Although there are
three trade associations, it remains totally unregulated by law.

In the nineteenth century, undertakers were carpenters and
transporters. Their establishment as funeral directors grew out
of a complex shift in attitudes to death which, during the
twentieth century, removed 'death' from the home and sought
to put it, sanitised, at arms' length.

The laying-out of the body was traditionally done by a
woman from the family or a local woman who often doubled
as a midwife. Midwifery, however, became a profession of its
own in the early twentieth century and increasingly, the
undertaker began to be firmly established as the person who
would take on all the arrangements following from a death.

Now the undertaker, professionalised into a funeral director,
has almost completely taken over the previous functions of
families and neighbours, as funerals have become more
sophisticated and materialistic.

Social and family bonds have loosened and we are
unfamiliar and apprehensive about death – all of which
encourages the use of a stranger who will come in and take
responsibility for everything. Funeral directors are no longer
tradesmen providing a simple service to a bereaved family; they
have become professionals, managers and consultants. They
have codes of practices, training, professional organisations and
qualifications.

There is no doubt that for many people who are shocked
d distressed following a death, the funeral director's
derstanding and familiarity with what needs to be done is a
t comfort and support: they mostly provide a valuable,
competent service.

Funeral directors today find themselves in a very difficult
position. Their background, practices and style have been
rooted in local communities where they have had a respected
role: there was a particular, comforting mystique about their
services. In our present more assertive, cynical and consumer-
conscious society, they are under more scrutiny. Their sombre,
dignified services are more transparent and we are much more
aware of their business practices: we know, these days, how to
work out the costs of things and funerals are much discussed
in terms of value for money.

Often the local funeral director had little business
competition and did not need to be commercially aggressive –
a ripe target for large national and international corporations
which have effectively swooped across the country swallowing
hundreds of small firms and tainting the whole trade with their
profit-led practices.

In Britain today there are four strands to the funeral
business.

◆ the National Association of Funeral Directors
◆ the Co-operative Funeral Service (CRS and CWS)
◆ Service Corporation International (SCI)
◆ Society of Allied and Independent Funeral Directors (SAIF).

Twenty years ago there was stability. Funeral directors were
mostly small, single, long-standing, family businesses, well
established and respected in their community. In the 1980s, an
enterprising businessman, Howard Hodgson, began to buy up
these independent firms, many of whom were lacking an
aggressive business sense and not 'maximising their trading
capacity'. He began by buying the family funeral business from
his father for £5,000: within a few years it was worth £8 million
and he had a large share of the market. Hodgson's firm is now
owned by a United States company – Service Corporation
International (SCI).

Service Corporation International (SCI)

Rather than sweep in with a new style and refurbished premises, this company has largely flourished behind the old-fashioned, comfortable reputations of old family firms, often retaining the former owner and staff.

The changes they *did* bring were to introduce aggressive sales practices. The result is that, in appearance, funeral directors and their offices seem largely unchanged, but we are beginning to have a sense of unease about some of their 'modern methods'.

SCI has 30 per cent of the French market, 25 per cent in Australia and a huge market in the United States. In Britain in 1998 it owned over 700 funeral firms – 15 per cent of the market.

Most funeral directors have only a few funerals a week. Their overheads, however, remain constant – premises, office staff, cars and hearses. SCI has rationalised all this. Their method is to target a large urban area and buy up a carefully chosen selection of the funeral businesses – mainly funeral directors but sometimes cemeteries, crematoria, even florists. These resources can then be 'clustered'. This means that the hearses, limousines, drivers, embalmers and administrative staff can be grouped centrally and serve half a dozen 'outlets', making massive savings.

Because they have saturated the area, there is little competition: a funeral is essentially a local operation and it is just not feasible to shop around 30 miles away. There is also no need to be competitive on prices and these begin to rise – by 5–6 per cent a year. Its business prospects are encouraging:

> *Aggregate deaths have increased at roughly 1.1 per cent on a compound basis since 1940....(this) should enable the death care industry to experience extremely stable demand in the future.*

Goldman Sachs

The National Association of Funeral Directors

The NAFD has had a code of practice for many years covering contentious issues such as the availability of full, detailed written information and complaints procedures. In particular, the code says that price lists should be readily available so that clients can make a free choice of the service they wish to have.

All the trade associations advocate the easy availability of what they call a 'basic funeral'. This should cost no more than £800 and consist of the following:

◆ provision of a simple coffin
◆ care of the deceased
◆ conveyance of the deceased
◆ provision of hearse and bearers
◆ making administrative arrangements.

(This will not cover things like church or crematorium fees, flowers, following car or embalming.)

Many funeral directors can supply this basic funeral for a total of £750 including a charge of just under £100 for a coffin. Firms controlled by SCI (UK) have a minimum charge of £285 for a coffin alone.

However, following a successful sales pitch the company maintains an average charge for a coffin of £500. These are not coffins of superior quality: they are the same as the ones provided for £100. Their cost price is £50.

The Society of Allied Independent Funeral Directors (SAIF)

SCI has brought much tension and hostility to funeral circles. The independent funeral directors who remain find mutual support and self-promotion in SAIF, which was set up in 1989 and now has 900 members nationally. Each member must have a satisfactory trading history, comply with the Society's code of practice, allow inspection of their premises and have complaints procedures. The Society is against unfair practices involving restriction of consumer choice and aggressive marketing.

SAIF basic funerals

For £750 (in the provinces) (plus fees) members of SAIF will provide a basic funeral. It includes:

◆ conveying the body to chapel of rest or elsewhere (two bearers)
◆ a basic coffin

- gown or own clothes
- visit to view body if required
- hygienic treatment (embalming)
- Hearse and one limousine, staff to supervise.

Extras can be quoted for – catering, extra cars, etc.

They will even provide a *really basic funeral* (as approved by DSS and Office of Fair Trading): hearse, no viewing, no embalming, no gown, transport to crematorium or cemetery, burial. Cost £500 maximum plus fees. (The fees are the fixed disbursements paid for medical certificates, crematorium or burial fees and a fee for a minister conducting the funeral service.)

You can get the name of a local SAIF member from:

- The Society of Allied and Independent Funeral Directors, Crowndale House, 1 Ferdinand Place, London NW1 8EE. Tel: (020) 7267 6777. Website: http://www.saif.org.uk/

How do they know what to do?

The NAFD provides a one-year course for funeral directors who can achieve a Diploma in Funeral Directing (Dip FD). This covers:

- the role and function of the funeral director in the community
- the National Association of Funeral Directors' Code of Practice
- health and safety
- communication skills
- personal attitudes to death
- the stages of grief which may be experienced
- a basic knowledge of client care
- administrative and business subjects.

There are also NVQs (levels 2 and 3) and BTECs which are much more practice based.

How much will a funeral cost?

> *Here lies one who for medicine would not give*
> *A little gold: and so his life is lost.*
> *I fancy that he'd wish again to live*
> *Did he but know how much his funeral cost.*
>
> Memorial in an Oxfordshire churchyard

How do you measure the value for money of a funeral? It is commonplace to spend several thousand pounds on a wedding – accepting the importance of the ritual and ceremony. However, we tend to think of the funeral cost in terms of the purchase of a simple coffin and charges for a hearse, minister, church or crematorium.

How do the charges break down?

1 pint of liquor for those who dived for him	*1s*
1 quart of liquor for those who brot him home	*2s*
2 quarts of wine and 1 gallon of cyder to jury of inquest	*5s*
8 gallons and 3 quarts wine for funeral	*£1.15s*
Barrel cyder for funeral	*16s*
1 coffin	*12s*
Windeing sheet	*1s*

1678 funeral bill for a man drowned at Hartford, Connecticut

When preparing this book I wrote to a dozen local funeral directors asking for information about charges. I had two helpful replies – from the Co-operative Funeral Service and an unconventional local firm. In spite of codes of practice, it has proved difficult to receive any hard information from High Street firms.

As a guide to what reasonable charges *can* be, here are the price lists of a couple of organisations concerned to offer a good deal to the public:

◆ **Carlisle Bereavement Service**, Cemetery Office, Richardson Street, Carlisle CA2 6AL. Tel: (01228) 625310. Fax: (01228) 625313, (Manager: Ken West)

This is a local authority cemetery and cremation department.

Coffins	£
Standard chipboard (oak finish)	116.00
Cardboard coffins	62.00

Cremation	£
Cremation of child (up to 1 month)	35.00
(1 month – 18 years)	57.00
Cremation over 18 years	235.00
Cremation (cardboard coffin)	210.00
Use of Chapel of Rest, 24 hrs	9.00
48 hrs–72 hrs	12.50–15.50
Postage of cremated remains (UK)	17.00
Metal urn	7.00
Provision of each bearer at service	6.00

Burial fees	
Interment of child up to 1 month	22.00
Interment of child: 1 month – 18 years	43.00
Interment over 18 years	208.00
Non-resident of Carlisle	229.00
Interment of cremated remains	58.00
Woodland grave	111.00
Use of burial chapel	32.00

In Carlisle there is no charge for keeping the body in the hospital mortuary before the funeral.

You will have to arrange the transport of the coffin from the hospital mortuary to the crematorium or cemetery. Local funeral firms will do this for £56.00–£100.00.

This means that in Carlisle you can arrange a complete funeral for between £500 and £600; £400–£500 if you use a cardboard coffin.

◆ **Wrekin Funeral Services**, 6 Whitchurch Rd, Telford TF1 3AG. Tel: (01952) 251125. (Manager: Suzanne Helm)

An organisation which trades like a funeral director, but which has been formed by a group of ex-local authority (cemetery department) officers to help people who wish to be more involved. You can choose from a menu which service you want and which to leave out.

Conveyance to funeral home	£60.00
Cheapest chipboard coffin	£180.00
Cardboard coffin	£90.00
Care and preparation	£60.00
Hearse for funeral	£120.00
Funeral director's services	£90.00

And then add the disbursements...

Normally the first quotation from funeral firms does not include 'disbursements', only the charge for their own services. They will pay them on your behalf and add them to the bill.

The NHS sets doctors' fees, and the Church Commissioners set the fees for funerals in church and burials and monuments in churchyards. Individual local authorities set their own charges in municipal cemeteries and crematoria.

Disbursements to the crematorium, cemetery, doctors, ministers or officiants are currently (1999) approximately:

Doctor's fee	£41	(each)
Crematorim fee	£180	(but varies)
Obituary notices	£42	
Service in church		
Minister's fee	£35	
Parochial Church Council	£29	
Service in crematorium		
Minister's fee	£64	
Burial in churchyard		
Parochial Church Council	£115	
Minister's fee	£23	

(There is no fee to the minister if the burial follows a service in church.)

When you add these to the NAFD costs quoted above, the 'basic' and the 'really basic' funerals will cost over £1,000 and over £800 respectively. (You can do without the obituary notice, but you may find yourself paying much more in cremation charges.) There will also be much more expense for a burial, and extra fees for a church service for heating, music (organist) and a verger.

See Appendix III for average funeral costs in different regions of the UK.

How to get ahead in funeral directing

I have nothing against undertakers personally. It's just that I wouldn't want one to bury my sister.

Jessica Mitford, 1964

In my local evening paper the six local funeral directors each have a 3" display panel advertisement – each headed by their logos. Such is local competition that these columns have become a battlefield for public attention: the principal weapon is the alphabet. The paper places advertisements in alphabetical order of the opening text (95 per cent of customers stick with the first funeral director they approach):

JOE BLOGGS 1
A. Baines, *White Street, Browntown*
Day and Night Service . . . Tel: . . .

JOE BLOGGS 2
A ban*d of dedicated professionals giving absolute attention to detail.*
A privately owned family firm . . . Tel: . . .

JOE BLOGGS 3
A Be*reavement Service. Conducted with dedication and commitment by the only independent family firm in the town . . . Tel: . . .*

JOE BLOGGS 4
A ca*ring, personal service with dignity and sympathy at all times.*
Private Chapel of Rest . . . Tel: . . .

JOE BLOGGS 5
A complete *funeral Service. Day or night.*
Throughout all areas . . . Tel: . . .

JOE BLOGGS 6
A complete quality *service to put your mind at rest.*
All areas covered. 24 HOUR SERVICE... Tel:...

Who pays for the funeral?

Funeral costs can be paid out of the estate of the dead person. The funds, however, are needed now and it will take some time for things to be sorted out – any bank accounts are automatically frozen at death. However, money can be released for immediate expenses on production of a death certificate.

There may be life insurance, trade union, professional association or occupational pension lump sums due. If the family has the resources, money can easily be found and reimbursed later. If expenses have not been planned for, however, there is the miserable prospect of raw grief being overlain with money worries and resentment. Does your next of kin know where to get £1,000 next week for your funeral?

Benefits Agency

If you receive Income Support, Jobseeker's Allowance, Family Credit, Housing Benefit, Council Tax Benefit or Disability Working Allowance and it is clear that you should be responsible for making funeral arrangements, you can apply for a Social Fund Funeral Payment. This will only cover a basic funeral and it will have to be repaid out of the estate.

The Benefits Agency will have a duty to ask whether any other close relative – parents, children, could take responsibility.

The health authority

The health authority may arrange for the funeral or cremation of someone who has died in hospital, if relatives either cannot be traced or are unable to pay. They will, nevertheless, lodge a claim for reimbursement from the estate.

The local authority

The local authority has a duty to bury or cremate the deceased if no other arrangements have been made. If they have reason to believe that there was a special wish to be buried this will be respected: otherwise a cremation will be arranged. Such funerals are not second-rate versions of a normal occasion: funeral directors, hearses and a formal respectful committal are involved – but at a basic level.

Pre-purchased funerals

I've always thought it curious that older people have had such a horror of a 'pauper's funeral' – it does not carry the same emotional weight with younger people. The historian Ruth Richardson in her book *Death, Dissection and the Destitute* has come up with an explanation: there is a 'race memory' of a time in the nineteenth century when dying in poverty was shameful not in itself but because of other implications.

Executed criminals' bodies had always been used for medical dissection because of the low availability of legally obtained bodies. In 1832, the Anatomy Act was passed which also allowed the use of bodies of people who had died 'on the parish' – destitute. To die, therefore, without the means for your burial meant the ignominy of possible involuntary dissection.

It was at this time that funeral clubs began to be established – early pre-payment funeral plans. Nowadays, poverty is less of a problem and even someone who is penniless will be provided with a basic funeral. However, the idea has lingered of paying for a funeral in advance so that any worry about money is out of the way.

There are other reasons why it might be a good idea:

◆ You can have what you want.
◆ You can relieve your next of kin of the burden.
◆ You can buy tomorrow's funeral at today's prices – although it remains a gamble whether that will be better than leaving your money where it is: but at least the bill is out of the way.

Nearly 200,000 people in Britain have bought pre-paid funerals costing, on average, £1,000 each (without disbursements) and this number is expected to rise to 500,000 by 2001. There are various ways of doing it:

◆ You can simply set aside a sum of money that is designated for your funeral.

◆ You can make an arrangement with an insurance company or funeral director who specialise in such things, fill in the forms and make the payments – leaving the details to your family when the time comes.

◆ If you want to be more involved, you can work out a detailed plan of the whole ceremony – including the type of coffin, music, readings and any other particular requirement.

If you want something different it is almost essential that you do some preparation to find out the possibilities and to leave detailed instructions about your wishes. If you can have these details settled in advance, it will save a lot of difficulty for someone who might otherwise be unfamiliar with unusual arrangements, perhaps at some distance from your home.

It's not necessarily as simple as arranging the payment of expenses. Even with a conventional funeral you may wish to leave instructions about, for example:

◆ Who will lay out your body? Some women will prefer a woman to do this – and men a man.

◆ Where do you want to be buried/cremated – do you need to buy a burial plot?

◆ What sort of service do you want (if any) – religious or secular?

◆ Who do you want to preside at the ceremony?

◆ What about the disposal of your cremated remains?

◆ Is it important to you that particular people are informed and invited (or excluded)?

◆ Have you any particular thoughts about what happens after the funeral – a small get-together or a larger celebration?

◆ Have you any strong feelings about flowers or a notice in the local newspaper?

These are things you will need to discuss with your family. It is, of course, vitally important that any arrangements you have made or would like are written down and known about by several people who will know immediately about your death. It will be most unhelpful for someone to recall 'I think he made some arrangement a few years ago with an undertaker in Leeds.'

Already the advantages become apparent, the main one being that your next of kin will not be haunted by doubts about whether they are 'doing the right thing'. It's a gift from you to them. And yet, only one in 50 British funerals every year is pre-paid.

If you do intend to buy a pre-paid plan it's worth shopping around and checking the fine details:

♦ What happens if your arrangement is with a funeral director in Ipswich and you subsequently move house to Glasgow?

♦ What happens if you die before the payments have been completed?

♦ What isn't included in the price? Cremation charges? Payments to the church?

Be careful...

Pre-payment plans are now a growing part of the funeral industry. They are worth £200 million a year and they are totally unregulated. It feels as though these plans should be subject to the same rigorous controls that exist in the insurance and travel business, but they are not.

If the company fails – and they have – you risk losing your whole investment.

In addition, when the time comes you might find that the plan does not cover incidental expenses such as crematorium charges and doctors' fees. It may also tie you to one particular firm with no possibility of a refund if you die outside their local area.

However, my impression is that things have improved considerably in the last few years and the industry seems to be tightening up – especially on arrangements for where funds are kept.

> It is interesting that in the nineteenth century, many of the early pre-burial plans were operated by publicans, who retrieved much of the benefits in the public bar after the funeral.

During the last few decades, there has been a trend for American ideas and business practices to migrate eventually to Britain. If this continues, a fixed-price pre-paid funeral might be a shrewd move. The United States NAFD did a survey in 1997 which revealed that the average cost of an American funeral was nearly £3,000. This didn't include cemetery or cremation charges, such as grave space or memorial stones. Any gathering for refreshments would also be extra.

In Britain the National Federation of Consumer Groups has been campaigning for a code of practice and an arbitrator who can receive complaints.

Most deaths occur within ten years of the arrangement being made and 90 per cent of pre-payment plans are being sold to people over 70 years on low incomes: their payments might be better spent on other things.

Shopping around might be something that you feel uncomfortable about. It might be a good idea to talk about it to a friend who could do the negotiating on your behalf: such a discussion might be very useful in helping you clarify your thoughts – and you can do the same for them.

On the other hand, many bereaved people find some comfort in having to focus on all the arrangements to be made and might prefer to do all the work themselves. Some people might see arranging the funeral as a final task they can do for the deceased. As with other things, it's best to discuss things with relatives and friends now.

The largest organisations offering pre-paid plans are:

◆ The Co-operative Funeral Bond. Tel: 0800 289120.
◆ Golden Charter. Tel: 0800 833800.
◆ Dignity in Destiny. Tel: 0800 269318.
◆ Chosen Heritage. Tel: 0800 525555.
◆ The Perfect Assurance Trust. Tel: (0121) 709 0019.
◆ Age Concern Funeral Plan. Tel: (01342) 327979.

What if you are dissatisfied with your funeral director?

If you have a complaint you should try to resolve it with the funeral director through their own procedures. They are likely to be a member of one of the trade associations, which you could also contact:

◆ National Association of Funeral Directors, 618 Warwick Road, Solihull, West Midlands B91 IAA. Tel: (0121) 711 1343.

◆ Society of Allied & Independent Funeral Directors, Crowndale House, 1 Ferdinand Place, London NWI BEE. Tel: (020) 7267 6777.

If you are not satisfied with the service you get, or the prices you are asked to pay, you should contact an advice centre such as the Citizens' Advice Bureau (CAB) or your local council's Trading Standards Department. The Funeral Ombudsman will investigate, free of charge, complaints made against funeral directors who are members of the Funeral Ombudsman Scheme:

◆ The Funeral Ombudsman, 26–28 Bedford Row, London WCIR 4HL.

Embalming and preparation

For my Embalming (sweetest) there will be
No spices wanted, when I'm laid by thee.

Anon

Embalming is a controversial procedure. Many funeral directors do it as a matter of course – 'unless asked not to' – so you must make your wishes known if you do not wish it to happen to you or someone else.

What happens?

Embalming involves draining the blood from the body and replacing it with formaldehyde, pumped into the circulatory system under pressure, injected into internal body cavities, under the skin or applied directly to the skin surface: this has a hardening and disinfecting effect.

A pinkish dye – safranine – is sometimes mixed with the formaldehyde to restore a lifelike, warm colour to the skin.

The body is undressed, cleaned and disinfected with a germicidal solution: any visible skin blemishes are removed with solvents. The hair is washed, the face is shaved and plastic eye-caps and a mouth former are inserted to fill out any deformity. Sometimes the cheeks can be filled out by injecting a mastic compound into the mouth. The throat and nose will have been packed with cotton gauze.

The mouth is closed either by stitching a thread through the lower and upper lips into the inside of the nose or using a barbed wire device inserted into the gums: a skilled embalmer will aim to preserve a lifelike, benign facial expression.

The head is raised above the level of the heart. Any stiffness from *rigor mortis* is relieved by the embalmer flexing and massaging the arms and legs, which are positioned so that there can be an easy flow of fluid through the circulation system.

Any deformation of limbs – perhaps caused by arthritis – is rectified by the use of splints or occasionally severing tendons or other tissue.

The face, neck and hands are covered with a thin layer of massage cream and the body is dressed in a tight-fitting plastic garment which will contain any leaking fluids.

A two-inch incision is made in the leg, the arm or, more usually, the neck. The femoral artery and vein (in the arm), the axillary artery and vein (in the armpit) or the carotid artery and vein (the neck) are pulled to the surface. A metal tube is inserted in (usually) the carotid artery – pointing towards the feet – and the other end is hooked up to an embalming machine.

A drain tube is inserted in the jugular vein, again pointing towards the feet; this tube drains into a waste sink. Three or four gallons of embalming fluid are forced into the carotid artery under five to ten pounds-per-square-inch of pressure pushing the blood through the circulatory system and expelling it through the tube exiting from the jugular vein.

The constituency of the embalming fluid will vary according to the body size, water content, age, degree of decomposition and temperature. It will also be important to take into account the disease from which the person died and the nature of any medication they were taking, which can have an important effect on the success of the process.

The flushing may be repeated two or three times to make sure that all of the vessels are thoroughly treated. The fluid reaches the head by a process of 'bypass circulation'. The whole process can be assisted by repositioning and massaging the body. An experienced embalmer will know visually and by touch when the body is fully embalmed.

After this a sharpened vacuum tube – a trocar – is inserted through the abdominal wall into the heart, stomach, lungs, bladder, intestines, liver and other organs. The machine is switched on and the organ contents – blood, urine, faeces etc. – are removed by suction.

One industry writer said of the procedure, 'Some embalmers almost appear to imagine themselves amateur fencers. Their idea of aspirating is to make very rapid thrusts and lunges with the trocar. In fact, the trocar has to remain long enough in any given position to allow time to build up vacuum to remove gases and liquids in the cavities.'

The embalmer then infuses about sixteen ounces of a very strong undiluted chemical preservative into the abdomen through a trocar and the same amount into the chest. The embalmer will often direct the trocar into the scrotum and penis of males who have not received adequate arterial embalming fluid.

Trocar holes are then sewn shut or closed with trocar buttons, bevelled plastic screws that are pushed into the holes. In bodies that have recently had surgery or been organ donors, the embalmer reopens incisions, aspirating organ contents and performing cavity embalming under direct view. He then sews the incision closed. If cavity aspiration and embalming are not done, it is likely that bowel contents will seep up through the mouth and nose. This seepage is known in the industry as 'purge'. In many funeral homes where embalmers do not routinely embalm the abdominal organs (cavity embalming), the embalmer places cotton under the pillow in the casket so the attendant can use it to wipe off 'purge' (dark liquid) that comes out of the mouth and nose.

A trocar can also be passed through the nose and into the skull through the thin bone at the top of the nose (cribiform plate). Early users of this method inserted the trocar alongside the nose at the corner of the eye ('the eye process'). Embalmers remove gas and fluid from the skull and instill cavity embalming fluid. They then pack the nose with cotton to avoid leaks.

Cavity embalming can also be used to preserve organs replaced in the chest or abdomen after an autopsy.

Kenneth V. Iserson, *Death to Dust* Galen Press 1994

It may be necessary to supplement this arterial embalming by injecting fluid into parts of the body the pump has not reached – the buttocks, chest, shoulders and abdominal wall. Injection alone may be sufficient for the embalming of foetuses and very young infants.

The structure of the body will now harden over an eight- to ten-hour period. It must be dressed and positioned because it will not be possible to move the limbs afterwards.

Embalming prevents decomposition for a short time – days, weeks. It stops the body smelling and it removes signs of trauma from the face. Sometimes cosmetics are used or facial damage is reconstructed as part of the process.

In other words... it makes the body look as though it is not dead. Not only that but a skilled embalmer will be able to make someone appear *exactly* as though they were asleep – causing emotional outbursts from distressed relatives – 'Why doesn't he wake up!' One funeral director I talked to said that although there is an appearance of 'health', there is an unnatural hardness to the touch which makes the dead person into an 'object' – as opposed to the soft flesh of the unenbalmed body.

Whether this is something you want is a matter for you. I don't wish to take away any comfort for distraught relatives: if this is going to be helpful to you, go ahead. However, many people find it an untruthful practice, which denies a reality from which they do not wish protection.

(There are occasions when embalming is wise – following liver or bowel cancer, for example, when decomposition may well have taken hold before death: it will then progress very rapidly and things could get very unpleasant without the embalmer's intervention.)

There is some growing environmental concern about cremation or burial involving formaldehyde which will eventually either seep into the ground or be emitted as a pollutant into the air. There can also be a tendency for the embalmer to use too much rather than too little fluid which can leak out through the skin and form a pool in the coffin.

Embalming is to make the corpse presentable for viewing in a suitably costly container.

Jessica Mitford, *The American Way of Death*

To reduce costs it would be appreciated if people trimmed the grass around their own graves.

NOTICE IN A
BRISTOL CEMETERY

CHAPTER 6

Disposal of the Body

'*I hate funerals.' That's what people say: nearly everyone. So why do we go to all to the trouble? For many bereaved people, the funeral is an ordeal to be endured. For others, not immediately bereaved, it is a rip-off.*

For clergy, it is a time for committing the deceased to God's care. Psychologists say it is a minor part of the grief process. Funeral directors, especially those in Australia and the United States, say it is a major part of the grief process; though for them it is also a way of making a living. For anthropologists, it affirms or creates social structure. In the eyes of some sociologists, it is a display of status and an atonement for guilt.

Tony Walter, *Funerals and How to Improve Them*

One of the most important things we should do, even if we are reluctant to become involved with the detailed arrangements, is to give some indication to our next of kin about how we want our body to be disposed of.

It seems wrong to leave such a personal decision to someone else – it's a matter of good manners.

Nobody can 'own' your body, but the executor (the person appointed in a will to administer your affairs after death) or your next of kin can be 'in possession' of it. In the absence of either of these, the State can assume possession. Whoever it is, curiously, they can dispose of your body however they like, although we ought to expect that our wishes be respected.

Strangely, the law is vague about whether it is actually obligatory to bury or cremate a body. Given that there is no health danger, it is possible that you might be able to keep a preserved, embalmed body legally at home.

If you want to...

Burial

Bury me not when I am dead.
Lay me not down in a dusty bed.
I could not bear the life down there
With earthworms creeping through my hair.

Memorial in a Connecticut churchyard

My Husband promised me
That my body should be
Cremated
But other influences prevailed

Memorial in an Ohio churchyard

All I desire for my own burial, is not to be buried alive; but
how or where, I think must be entirely indifferent to every
rational creature.

Lord Chesterfield, *Letters*, 1769

Traditionally, in Western culture, bodies have been disposed of by burial. A *permanent* grave, however, is a relatively modern idea. Before the nineteenth century death and burial were commonplace, bodies were buried in shrouds and memorials were simple wooden crosses; it was natural that such impermanent graves should be re-used in time – bones were simply gathered together and reburied.

With the rise of greater class divisions, people wanted to express their status with grander coffins and elaborate gravestones and memorials. There were problems, however, following the population surge at the beginning of the nineteenth century: churchyards began to fill up.

From the 1830s onwards, local authorities and private companies began to open large cemeteries like those at Highgate and Kensal Green. Cemetery burial began to be seen as an indication of status. Nowadays, although you have a right to be buried in the graveyard of your local parish church if you are a resident of the parish, because of lack of space this is usually impossible – although there are variations from parish to parish.

The usual place for burial for most people will be a cemetery run by a local authority. These usually have consecrated spaces for members of the Church of England or other religious denominations. There will be a non-denominational chapel where any kind of religious or secular service can be performed before the burial.

Many people consider their grave to be a private, permanent place. This is not always the case. In churchyards one grave may contain several coffins, buried over the years, and there is usually a time limit – say 75 years – on the period during which it will remain undisturbed. After that, however, the graves may be moved and used again (skeletal remains being reburied). It is unusual (and very expensive) to have an exclusive, permanent, private churchyard grave.

All graves in local authority cemeteries before 1977 have perpetuity rights. There is currently (1999) discussion about changes to allow re-use: a concept called 'lift and deepen':

> *The Home Office is issuing a consultation document on this any day now. It would create the legislation to allow us to open 'private' and public graves at least 100 years old, place any bones in a wood box, and re-inter them below six feet, which would allow two new burials. These burials would be turned round so that the headstone could be placed at the head end, leaving the existing memorial in position. We would have to advertise such proposals, and people interested in retaining their family 'private' grave could do so, upon some agreed payment. Other measures would protect environmental aspects, historical graves, etc.*
>
> Ken West, Carlisle Bereavement Services

The costs involved in funerals and churchyard burials can be high. Apart from paying for the funeral and the grave you may also have to pay the minister and the Parochial Church Council for their services, facilities and permissions.

Because of the pressure on places in cemeteries – London is likely to run out of space in 10 to 15 years – new developments are afoot.

Service Corporation International (SCI) is beginning to move into the cemetery business. So far it has specialised in buying up small family funeral directors' businesses and crematoria. Now it sees the prospect of the grave crisis forcing the government's hand: it is unlikely that they will have any option but to agree to allow the over-full cemeteries to be redeveloped by allowing more aggressive grave re-use.

SCI has received planning permission in London, Leatherhead and Birmingham for another idea: above-ground mausoleums. The first one – in Streatham – will hold 260 bodies. There is talk of a permanent space in such a mausoleum, likely to cost over £8,000 and a whole family section (10–12 spaces) costing over £100,000.

There is an attraction for many people who wish to be neither cremated nor buried: their body will be 'safe'. However, you and I know that decomposition comes from inside: there's no escape.

Local authorities could see the sale of their cemeteries as an unexpectedly useful source of income. If the government agrees to more flexible re-use of graves, private companies could be in for a bonanza.

Cedric Mimms, in his book *When We Die*, makes the point that, because we tend generally to be very close to neither great grandchildren nor great grandparents, there would be some sense in making graves 'anonymous' after two to three generations so that they could be re-used.

Cemetery: an isolated suburban spot where mourners match lies, poets write at targets and stone cutters spell for a wager.
Ambrose Bierce, *The Devil's Dictionary*

Cremation

'It nearly conceals my fear of death,' my dearest said, 'When I think of cremation. To rot in the earth is a loathsome end, but to roar up in flames – besides, I am used to it. I have flamed in love or fury so often in my life. No wonder my body is tired, no wonder it is dying. We had great joy of my body. Scatter the ashes.'
Robinson Jeffers, 1963

There has been a shift in public attitudes over the last 150 years. The traditional churchyard burial had an association in people's minds with the idea of 'resurrection'. However, the increase in the population has meant that burial space has been severely limited and has consequently increased in cost. We have also become more aware of the public health risk of infection and we find the idea of a rotting corpse repugnant. Because of this we have been drawn to the hygienic, cleansing crematorium.

Cremation was not legal in Britain until the late nineteenth century; it was considered a barbaric, pagan ritual. It is still forbidden to Orthodox Jews and Muslims. The Roman Catholic Church has allowed its members to be cremated only since the 1950s. It is obligatory for adult Hindus.

The first cremation was in 1885: in 1902 there were only seven crematoria in the whole country and 431 cremations compared to half a million burials. In 1939, 4 per cent of funerals used cremation, but there was a rapid growth after 1945.

Now the figure is 70 per cent in England and Wales (50 per cent in Scotland). Only Japan (97 per cent) prefers cremation more than us. There is a wide difference in national attitudes to cremation depending on the strength of their Catholic influence and the amount of space available for burial. In Belgium (a densely populated country) 20 per cent of funerals are cremations and in France (lots of space and widely Catholic) the proportion is 12 per cent. In Spain the proportion is 4.7 per cent and in Italy an amazing 1.5 per cent. In 1997 in Britain there were 640,000 deaths and 446,000 cremations.

When Jessica Mitford wrote *The American Way of Death* in 1963 only 3.71 per cent of US funerals ended in cremation: now it is 21 per cent.

In the past, there was some suspicion of the complete destruction by fire because of the belief in bodily resurrection and the fear that the removal of physical evidence would be an encouragement to poisoning.

The process of cremation

Within the cremator a single burner is placed at one end and fires diagonally down onto the hearth. The aim is to consume the coffin and its contents as efficiently and quickly as possible with the minimum of smoke and other emissions. To do this requires a temperature of between 800°C and 1000°C. The cremation chamber is full of flame – the actual incineration cannot be seen.

The burning is aided considerably by the combustion of the coffin and body: a 10-stone body in a 6-stone coffin will generate a massive 800,000 BTU of heat. A supply of air is needed for efficient and complete combustion and if thick black smoke is to be avoided: how much air is a matter for judgement, depending on the material in the coffin, the obesity of the body and the operating temperature of the cremator.

Under recent EU legislation all crematoria have to comply with stringent regulations about their construction, to reduce environmental pollution. Nevertheless, pollutants – mercury, formaldehyde – do escape and continue to be a cause for concern.

W. E. D. Evans in his book, *The Chemistry of Death*, describes the process of combustion:

> *The coffin is introduced into the furnace where it rapidly catches fire, bulges and warps, and the coffin sides may collapse and fall, exposing the remains to the direct effect of the flames. The skin and hair at once scorch, char and burn . . .*
>
> *The muscles slowly contract, and there may be a steady spreading of the thighs with gradually developing flexion of the limbs. . . . Occasionally there is swelling of the abdomen before the skin and abdominal muscles char and split; the swelling is due to the formation of steam and the expansion of gases in the abdominal contents.*
>
> *Destruction of the soft tissues gradually exposes parts of the skeleton. The skull is soon devoid of covering, then the bones of the limbs appear, commencing at the extremities of the limbs where they are relatively poorly covered by muscle or fat, and the ribs also become exposed. The small bones of the fingers, wrists and ankles remain united by their ligaments for a surprising length of time, maintaining their anatomical relationships even though the hands and feet may fall away from the adjacent long bones.*

The abdominal contents burn fairly slowly, and the lungs
more slowly still....The brain is specially resistant to complete
combustion...Eventually the spine becomes visible as the
viscera disappear, the bones glow whitely in the flames and the
skeleton falls apart.

W. E. D. Evans, *The Chemistry of Death*, Springfield 1963

The process will take a couple of hours (depending on the size
of the coffin and body), plus time for the remains to cool. A
thin body will take longer than a body that has a thicker layer
of combustible fat.

There have been concerns that harmful quantities of mercury
dental fillings could escape with the other gases, mercury being
a volatile substance. Tests show that all the mercury is indeed
released and, allowing for five amalgam fillings per head in
the 70 per cent of us who still have their own teeth, about 11
kg of mercury would exit each year from an average-sized
crematorium doing 3,500–4,000 cremations. Evidently this
matter merits attention, perhaps mercury (and silver) could be
recovered during the incineration process....

During busy periods more than one coffin is processed at a
time, but the remains are kept strictly separate. Initially they
contain small fragments of incinerated bone, together with
metallic objects from rings, tooth fillings, artificial hips or
coffin nails. The metallic objects are removed with an
electromagnet and the rest pulverised so that it is truly in the
form of fine ashes. In Britain about 40,000 hip replacement
operations are performed each year, and there are metal
residues in up to three-quarters of all cremations. Unexpected
metal items have included coins, surgical forceps and scissors, a
micrometer and a ring cutter!

Cedric Mims, *When We Die*, Robinson 1998

The residue will be a mixture (about 50 per cent) of coffin ash
and human 'cremains' – the high temperatures involved will
consume a wooden coffin almost completely. What remains are
mostly small white bone fragments and residua. There may be
tinges of pale colouring caused by the presence of iron, gold
rings, other jewellery or dental fillings.

The bony remains are then pulverised in a cremulator, which grinds the pieces into the 'ashes' – about the size and consistency of granulated sugar. Apart from the powdered bone, the body tissues will have been reduced to their main chemical constituents – calcium, sodium, nitrogen, potassium and phosphorus. The ashes will weigh about 4 per cent of the original body weight – usually about 2 kg.

The ritual of cremation does not allow people to see the body put to its final resting-place as a burial does – the coffin disappears. However, you can choose in advance – and imaginatively – how you want your ashes to be disposed of. They can be scattered in the crematorium garden of remembrance or some other place that is meaningful to you. You can also have them buried in a churchyard or cemetery if it's important to identify a definite location.

In the case of babies and very young children, because of the incomplete bone formation, there may be no ashes following a cremation. (There is something incredibly distressing about this – with adults there is, at least, some tangible evidence of their existence.)

There are fewer crematoria than cemeteries and churchyards: choosing cremation might be difficult in terms of how far you may need to travel. They also tend to operate only on weekdays, which might be another problem. (Apparently funeral directors and the clergy are opposed to weekend funerals.)

All too often crematoria have been dismal, unwelcoming places. However, there is evidence that they are becoming much more flexible than they used to be about offering choice to users. There is a move away from the rushed 20-minute conveyor-belt experience. There may be scope for planning how you want to use the space – maybe with seating less formally around the coffin.

It's usually possible, if wished, to be present when the coffin enters the cremator (this is an important part of Hindu practice). Crematorium managers are also generally helpful about supporting your own ideas for a funeral ceremony and welcome family enquiries. There is often a Chapel of Remembrance where a record is kept of individual cremations.

Friends or relatives can buy memorial stone plaques which

are displayed for a period of years (renewable) on memorial walls. Recently computer technology is bringing video screens into some crematoria where you can recall a personalised memorial on screen by using a personal swipe-card.

There is a wide range of prices for various services at different crematoria. Within 40 miles of each other near where I live, one allows 40 minutes for a service and charges £165.00 and another charges £200.00 for a 20-minute slot.

The 1990 Environmental Protection Act has had important implications for crematoria. Much more stringent regulations about emissions mean replacement of cremators and other equipment before the deadline of 1999. Worcester Crematorium, for example, is spending £800,000 on improvements, which will increase efficiency, reduce pollution and speed the cremation process from two hours to 70 minutes. How far this will become reflected in increased charges to users is unclear.

Which cemetery? Which crematorium?

We would never dream of asking a travel agent to arrange a holiday for us without looking at brochures from different travel companies, comparing prices and weighing up what was on offer. Yet very few of us show the same interest in planning a funeral: we usually leave it to a funeral director to arrange a standard package.

Robert Coates, the manager of Mortlake Crematorium – one of the busiest in London – was quoted in *The Guardian* (5 November 1997):

> *There is so much help we can give people and, yet, I reckon to get only seven calls a year at most. It's such a shame when they only discover afterwards that they could have done things differently, had a bit more choice or avoided some aspect of the ceremony which they'd rather have done without.*
>
> *It's tempting for the bereaved to think: 'let the professionals handle it, I know nothing about funerals.' But by contacting us first they can discover the range of choices available and then give their own instructions to a funeral director.*

In 1997 *The Directory of Cemeteries and Crematoria* by Martin Wainright was published. This lists the full range of sites – 220 crematoria and 2,000 cemeteries. It includes large and small, modest and grand facilities, including 'green' cemeteries. It's put together by the Cemetery Research Group at York University. It covers the law about burials, the restrictions you can find about headstones and the various options offered by crematoria. The *Directory* was written with consumers in mind – a sort of *Which?* report. Ask for it in your local reference library.

Another guide to 'best buys' is the *Natural Death Handbook*, published by the Natural Death Centre (see page 156), which gives full details about choices and costs.

Gravestones and memorials

> *ALLWOOD OCTUPLETS MAY BE EXHUMED OVER HEADSTONE ROW Mandy Allwood, who lost her octuplets after a series of miscarriages in October 1996, has applied to exhume their bodies from West Norwood Cemetery in London after Lambeth Council refused to allow the words 'Mummy' and 'Daddy' on the headstone.*
>
> Funeral Director, July 1998

It is important to many people not only that someone who has died should continue to live on in their memories, but that their death should be publicly marked in some material way. This may take many forms but traditionally a headstone on the grave is the preferred option.

Ordering a stone for a grave may be involved in the arrangements for the funeral but this is usually unwise. The filled grave should be allowed to settle before adding the stone and this may take several months.

It is also wise to allow some time to elapse before deciding what exactly is wanted. There are likely to be a limited range of shapes, materials and sizes that are acceptable and available, so you should talk to your local stonemason who will know the particular requirements of local churches and cemeteries.

It is likely that cemetery and church authorities will also have clear opinions about what wording you can use – 'reverential and respectful', rather than informal or whimsical.

You will have to pay over £300 for an average gravestone: and that's just for the stone. The more words, the more expensive – like a very robust telegram. The following are typical prices (and you need to add VAT).

Headstone	£300.00
Inscription	£1.20 (per word)
Permission to erect	£98.00 (churchyard)
Permission to erect	£73.00 (cemetery)
Erection	£80.00

Crematoria have memorial walls in their grounds where stone plaques can be placed for a (renewable) period of years. You can also usually have a rose bush planted (depending on available space). This is likely to be expensive as it includes a charge for ground maintenance.

More and more people are using the Internet to post memorials – headstones from cyberspace (see also Appendix VII). Have a look at Lauria Memorials at *www.lauriamemorials. com* for a sample of the (some would say, sentimental) style.

> *The tombstone is about the only thing that can stand upright and lie on its face at the same time.*
>
> Mary Wilson Little

A Methodist lay preacher is establishing Britain's first on-line cemetery. After an advertisement in *Funeral Service Journal* there were more than 100 enquiries from funeral directors. The personalised Internet epitaph consists of a photograph, a 1,000 word obituary and a copy of the death certificate. Interviewed in *The Guardian* (14 August 1997), David Wilkinson from Clevedon (near Bristol), whose idea it is, said:

> *We are seeking to bring back the dignity to funerals. This way you get a record of someone's life. In 100 years time, historians will welcome it.*

Sorting out the estate

The executor – named in the will – is in charge of dealing with the deceased's affairs.

If no one was named, or there was no will made, someone will have to apply for letters of administration. This process puts someone in the same position as an executor – except that they will be called the administrator.

Whether executor or administrator, they are the personal representative of the person who has died. They are responsible for paying all the deceased's debts, taxes and expenses, including funeral expenses. They make the payments from the estate not from their own income or savings. Only when these duties are finished can the personal representative share out the rest of the estate.

Probate

If you are a personal representative you may have to apply to prove the will: probate. This will give official confirmation of your power to deal with the estate and to pay the bills.

There are good reasons for probate:

◆ It looks after the interest of the deceased's creditors.
◆ It protects the interests of any surviving dependants.
◆ It checks that the estate will be distributed correctly.

Probate is not always necessary – it depends on the size of the estate. Normally, if the sums involved are small, organisations like the Post Office, banks or insurance companies are helpful and don't require the production of evidence of probate. However, if there are considerable sums involved, they will almost certainly wish to see the grant of probate or letters of administration.

The person who applies for a grant of probate should be over 18 and can be any one of the named executors. If there is a will but no named executor, it should be the main beneficiary. If there's no will, it should be the next of kin, in this order:

◆ the surviving spouse
◆ a child of the deceased (or a grandchild if there are no living children)
◆ a parent of the deceased
◆ a brother or sister of the deceased
◆ another relative of the deceased.

It is not necessary to employ a solicitor, but you should be aware that the handling of complicated estates can become a very onerous and responsible business. It is at this stage when you become very grateful (or otherwise) for the orderliness of the dead person's affairs.

You can apply to the nearest Probate Registry office to where you live – not necessarily the one local to the deceased. You will be sent further information and a series of forms to complete.

After all your enquiries and research you will be ready to complete the documentation – death certificate, will, bank account details, etc. and application – which is put together and sent to the Probate Registry.

In due course you will be asked to meet with a probate officer to go through the documentation and to sort out any problems: it should be fairly informal – not an 'investigation'.

Then the probate officer will let the personal representative know whether there is a tax liability – particularly for inheritance tax. You will also be asked to pay a probate fee (another testamentary expense). This will not come to more than a few hundred pounds for the largest estate.

The grant of probate or letters of administration will not be made until any outstanding tax bill has been paid – you have six months to do this (in instalments or in full).

For a small fee you should get some copies of the document as they will be required before funds will be released. When all the expenses, debts and taxes have been paid, the personal representative may then distribute anything left of the estate according to the will or the intestacy rules.

Claims on the estate

Whether someone is related or not, they can apply for a share of the estate if they were being supported financially in any way by the person who died, immediately before the death.

If they qualify they must apply within six months of the date on which probate or letters of administration are taken out. The court can allow later application in special circumstances. Get legal advice on how to do this. Don't be rushed into parting with goods before taking legal advice. Hire purchase goods cannot be repossessed after a third of the purchase price has been paid unless the firm gets a court order.

Where a deceased partner has left a debt, you may need to check with an advice centre or a solicitor about any liability for the debt.

Legal aid and advice

If you have any difficulty in dealing with the deceased's property, possessions or guardianship of their children, get advice from a solicitor or Citizens' Advice Bureau as soon as possible. Get the leaflets *Legal Aid Guide* and *Getting Legal Help* from a Citizens' Advice Bureau, public library, police station or a court, to find out if you can get legal aid.

These places also hold a list of local solicitors, which shows whether they take legal aid work and if they specialise in probate.

Many solicitors are prepared to give up to half an hour of legal advice for a small fee. You can get this fixed fee interview whether or not you qualify for legal aid.

Names of solicitors who give a fixed fee interview are in the *Solicitors' Regional Directory*, which you can find at local libraries, Citizens' Advice Bureaux and courts.

Welfare benefits following a death

Help for widows

As a widow there are different kinds of payments you can get depending on your age and the number of children you have living with you. The amount you can get is based on your husband's National Insurance contributions.

If you were not married but lived as though you were married, no matter how you might justly feel like one, you are *not* a widow and you do not qualify for widows' benefits. There is also no specific, corresponding help for widowers at present.

Widows' payment

When your husband dies you may get a Widows' Payment.

This is a tax-free lump sum – currently £1,000 – paid as soon as you are widowed (if your husband had paid enough National Insurance contributions, and either of you is under retirement age).

Widowed Mothers' Allowance

You may be able to get Widowed Mother's Allowance if you are already claiming Child Benefit or if you are expecting your husband's child (or are pregnant as a result of artificial insemination or in vitro fertilisation).

Increased allowances

If either you or your spouse were getting Retirement Pension, Incapacity Benefit, Child Benefit or Industrial Injury Benefit when they died, you may be eligible for an increased rate.

Help for guardians of your children

If someone is entitled to Child Benefit for a child they take into their family, they can also claim Guardian's Allowance.

Normally both parents of the child must be dead, but the allowance may sometimes be paid where only one has died and they were divorced or never married (or where the surviving parent is in prison or cannot be traced). They do not have to be the child's legal guardian.

Income Support

Income Support is a social security benefit for people aged 16 or over whose income is below a certain level.

You may be able to claim it if you are not expected to sign on as a jobseeker and you are, for instance:

- incapable of work due to sickness or disability, *or*
- bringing up children on your own, *or*
- aged 60 or over, *or*
- looking after a person who has a disability or registered blind.

You cannot normally get Income Support if you are working for 16 hours or more a week or if you have a partner (spouse or someone you live with as if you are married to them) who works 24 or more hours a week.

You can get Income Support on top of other benefits or on top of earnings from part-time work. If you have over £3,000 in savings the benefit will be reduced proportionately.

Receiving Income Support is a passport to other benefits that could add value to your income.

You may have to pay tax on some social security benefits.

The Benefits Agency publishes a very useful guide, *What To Do After A Death in England and Wales*, which you can get free from any of their offices. It sets out all the details in a very readable and clear way.

Changes to come

At the time of writing (1999) there are plans to change state benefits for bereaved families. From April 2001, there will be three major reforms:

◆ For the first time men will be eligible for Bereavement Benefits (as they will be called). However, they also must have been married to their partners and the payments (which will be increased) will be calculated according to their wife's contribution record.

◆ If the bereaved spouse is over the age of 45 and is without dependent children, the benefit will be paid for six months only – instead of until the age of 60.

◆ The present Widows' Payment of £1,000 will be doubled to £2,000 but paid only if the spouse died before reaching retirement pension age. This should at least keep pace with the realistic cost of funerals.

Although these changes may have been motivated by a wish to make savings (estimated at £500 million), there is nevertheless a sense of justice about them. There is recognition that the needs of bereaved people are common to both men and women and that, for the most part, the effects of loss are temporary. The emphasis moves to the urgent need for help with immediate, substantial funeral costs and changed expenses. Until now the low but lifelong pensions paid to widows have only confirmed them as 'helpless' and 'bereft' without the defining identity of their lost partner.

CHAPTER 7

Home Organised Funerals

O ur unwillingness to face the deaths of those around us means that, when it happens, the loss is keener and we become shocked: we are unable to think or act clearly. The conventional funeral organisation works well: we have a skilled funeral director, who knows what he's doing, to remove all the burden of planning the funeral and seeing to all the form-filling. This is often exactly what's needed and many people are rightly grateful. However, more and more, people are seeing the value of taking more control of planning what will happen after their own death and that of the person to whom they are closest.

Doing it yourself

The public perception has been that only experienced professionals are capable of dealing with arrangements following a death: 'they provide the best service' and who wouldn't want just that for their loved ones. Not to use a funeral director may feel like getting an amateur to rewire your house or doing your own conveyancing.

However, increasingly, people wish to play a more imaginative and intimate role in a family funeral, as we shall see later.

There are several advantages:

◆ The biggest is that you can arrange things exactly as you wish.

◆ You can avoid the depersonalised off-the-peg feel of many funerals.

◆ You can avoid any unnecessary expense and extravagance.

However, it is not advisable to make the decision to do it yourself at the time of someone's death. Unless you are strongly committed to the idea and have put time, thought and research into it you are unlikely to be satisfied with the result.

Doing it ourself may mean:

- Laying-out and preparing the body.
- Getting a coffin and placing the body in it.
- Storing the body until the funeral.
- Transporting the body to a mortuary if you are not keeping it at home.
- Booking a cremation or a burial.
- Organising a funeral service or ceremony.
- Arranging transport to the crematorium or cemetery.
- Carrying the coffin into the crematorium or at the cemetery.

This is not to say that a widow or widower or other main mourner should be involved in all this unaided: friends and family will be willing to help – indeed it won't work unless you have support. You may also be able to use a funeral director for some of the arrangements, although they are often unwilling to take on less than the whole job.

However, it's important that one person should co-ordinate things and take the risk that everything will go as planned. None of us are likely to have done this before, we only have one chance and the potential for mistakes is high. However, most people who do it would not have had it any other way.

> *If we complain about the cost of funerals, it is because we look at the work involved – transporting coffins and bodies – and conclude that it is not very onerous. We are correct – it is the kind of thing we could easily do ourselves. But we are rarely prepared to do it ourselves, and there's the rub.*
>
> Tony Walter, *Funerals and How To Improve Them*

The Natural Death Handbook

If you are planning a do-it-yourself funeral, *The Natural Death Handbook* makes very good background reading. This is published by the Natural Death Centre: it's a highly practical guide to the options available. There is also a massive list of funeral directors, crematoria and cemeteries giving details of their facilities. Further details from:

◆ The Natural Death Centre, 20 Heber Road, London NW2 6AA. Tel: (020) 8208 2853. Fax: (020) 8452 6434.

Preparing the body

See Appendix II for details of what this entails. It is a straightforward procedure but few people will find this an easy task so soon after death. Many people, however, take some comfort from being able to do this last service themselves – maybe there is a family member or friend who could help.

Perhaps the best solution is to find out how to get assistance from a local community nurse.

Registering the death

From reading the section on Registration (page 111) you will know that this can be complicated. You'll need to know where the Registrar's office is, when you can go and what information you need to take with you: perhaps someone else could take care of this for you.

(Doing the research and gathering all the information regarding the registration of your own death would be a kindness for the future.)

Storing the body

After a couple of days the body will begin to decompose unless it is kept cold: the rate of decomposition will vary according to the age of the deceased and the cause of death.

The easiest solution to this is to arrange for it to be stored at a hospital mortuary – if they are willing.

Some funeral directors may be willing to store a body for a few days for a charge of about £20 a day (*The Natural Death Handbook* gives a list of addresses).

If you wish to keep the body at home until the funeral you will need to use the coldest part of the house. Further cooling can be achieved with ice cubes or dry ice (obtained from the British Oxygen Company) packed in plastic bags and placed around the torso. You may be able to use electric fans or hire a portable air-conditioning unit. Another (unconventional) solution would be to construct a plastic tent around the body taped around the front of a fridge or upright freezer with the door removed.

Sometimes administrative complications mean that a funeral cannot take place for some weeks. This will mean that you will be unable to keep the body at home and you may have to compromise your independence. Perhaps the only way of slowing down the decomposition is to have the body embalmed, however reluctant you may be to do this. You may be able to find a funeral director who would be willing to provide this single service.

Acquiring a coffin

> *The man that made it didn't want it.*
> *The man that bought it had no use for it.*
> *The man who used it didn't know it.*
>
> Traditional riddle

Getting hold of a coffin used to be the main objection to do-it-yourself funerals. Only a few years ago it was all but impossible to buy one: now it is less of a problem. However, you're going to have to do some planning.

You will need to have researched the feasibility of getting a coffin delivered very quickly – within hours. Alternatively, you could get it well in advance of the need arising for its use, if you have somewhere to store it – they take up a lot of space. However, the image of a coffin is a potent one and many people will hesitate about its presence suspended from the roof inside the garage.

There will also be choices to be made about what sort of coffin to buy: some are expensive, some are enormous, some are basic and some are cardboard.

Surprisingly, the material in chipboard coffins, after burial, breaks down after only about four weeks which is quicker than a cardboard coffin. Both are biodegradable except that chipboard contains resins and formaldehyde, which are pollutants and will not break down.

Coffin suppliers

If you want to buy a coffin in advance you can do no better than to look in *The Natural Death Handbook* which will give a range of sources across the country. However, the following suppliers will give you an idea of what is available at what price:

◆ Heaven on Earth, Kingsley House, Cotham Road, South Kingsdown, Bristol BS6 5TZ. Tel: (0117) 942 1836 or 942 0972.

Heaven on Earth offers a range of funeral services. The fact that they do not describe themselves as 'funeral directors' reflects the importance they place on customer choice. They were awarded the Best Funeral Shop Award from the Natural Death Centre in 1997.

They seem to be willing to help to arrange exactly what is wanted by someone planning their own prospective funeral or bereaved family members.

They will supply a range of individual coffins made in a variety of materials, decorated or plain. They will give a little assistance if required or they will take complete charge. They are interested in 'creative' celebrations but would be happy to organise a conventional funeral. (They will do a full basic funeral for £550 plus disbursements.)

You can get a good idea of their range from their brochure (1999):

◆ Cotham Strandboard coffin chest without moulding £130
◆ Reclaimed timber coffin   £399
◆ Conventional coffins (unvarnished/can be painted)
  Veneered oak coffin   £175
  Veneered oak casket   £199
◆ Wicker coffins   £499
◆ Painted coffins (made from 0 per cent formaldehyde fibreboard)
  Coffins   £295
  Chests   £350
  Any of the above stencilled with one of Heaven on Earth's stencils   £75

- Bookcase coffins/chests
  Including discreet brass brackets   £350
  Shelves, each (made as furniture)   £8
- Collapsible shroud coffins (suitable only for burial)   £150
- Woollen shrouds and ropes   £115

They can supply all the conventional funerary handles and accoutrements for the coffin but prefer natural hemp/rope handles which cost £8 each. These are only necessary if you require a burial.

All linings are made from cotton and can be fitted from £35.00.

- Compakta, 2 Newbold Road, Desford, Leicestershire LE9 9GS. Tel/Fax: (01455) 828642.

This is the leading manufacturer of cardboard coffins in Britain.

Strength is achieved by using a design that relies on bending and folding and using several layers of thin board rather than a thick one. It can be folded together rather than using fasteners such as staples or bolts or other types of fixings which in themselves are not 'environmental'. It is easy to assemble and can contain any leaked body liquids if necessary.

There is naturally some resistance from funeral directors who see profit margins eroded, although nowadays it is much easier to obtain one.

Compakta Limited now produces:

- a white coffin suitable for decoration
- a woodgrain effect coffin for a traditional look
- pillows for standard coffins
- small coffins for non-viable foetal remains
- containers for transporting caskets of cremated remains.

The cardboard coffin is constructed from four separate sections that interlock to form a very strong structure. Whilst it takes only a few minutes for those familiar with the procedure to erect, it is better to buy it ready made – it's more manageable.

The empty coffin, whilst very strong, is also very light and can easily be carried (empty) by one person. There are six simple loop handles fitted to make carrying easier. They've been tested by suspending one by four of the handles containing a weight of 125 kg.

To maintain a clean appearance and enable long-term storage, the coffin is packed in a plain board box. The cost price to the funeral trade is under £40.00 (plus delivery), so bear this in mind when someone (and this really happened) tries to sell you one for £200.

The price to the public of the white coffin (direct from the factory) is £69.32 (including VAT) (1999). Delivery in England by 48-hour courier is an extra £12.93 including VAT – a total cost of £82.25 delivered. The woodgrain coffin costs £83.37 delivered. If you ring them before lunchtime, you'll get your coffin the following day. Delivery to Scotland costs extra.

I suggested that the word 'cardboard' has associations of cornflake packets and second-rate, shoddy material: could another description be given to what is, in fact, a high-quality product? Apparently not. 'Cardboard' is the accurate technical description and to call it anything else would contravene trading regulations.

Instead of decorating it to soften its rather bleak appearance it could also be covered with a decorated fabric pall.

> See Appendix V for some guidelines on making your own coffin.

Pacemakers

It's important to know whether the deceased has been fitted with a pacemaker, which *must* be removed – not necessarily needing medical skill. These can be very troublesome as they contain lithium batteries that will explode in a cremator. Funeral directors are responsible for the correct preparation of all materials entering the cremator and a mistake on your part could be costly:

Doctors were blamed yesterday for causing two serious explosions in crematoriums by leaving heart pacemakers in bodies. In one blast at the crematorium in Morden, Surrey, the damage cost £5,000 to repair.

Yesterday the cremation industry and local government said the explosions were widespread and that new European Union rules will make them more dangerous. After seven years of complaining, the Association of Metropolitan Authorities and crematorium operators complained of government inaction.

Anthony Wilson, Deputy Superintendent of Morden Crematorium, said, 'Doctors should be responsible for removing the pacemakers: they are most reluctant to accept this responsibility.' He added, 'EC rules will change the structure of cremators, so that any explosion won't be able to go up the chimney, but be blocked by an extra chamber where smoke is to be burnt off.'

The Guardian, 10 August 1996

Transport

People want dignity and gravitas, but prefer the look of a Volvo. It is not necessarily appropriate to have a cortège of Rolls Royces, except in Leicester and the West Midlands.

SCI Customer Research

We make a strong association between the transport of a coffin and the traditional hearse. It is not easy to find an alternative with which we can feel totally comfortable.

A large estate car may have room but seems too casual and may be difficult to hire: there are not many able to accommodate the bulk of a coffin. A van is easy to obtain but not one without 'Armstrong's Pies & Sausages' or 'Acme Van Hire' displayed on the side: they're for the transport of 'goods' and they have a feeling of being 'second best'.

You may be lucky and find a funeral director willing to hire out a hearse for the funeral but otherwise, you may need to swallow your discomfort and make the best of what's available.

Booking a cremation or a burial

This should be done as soon as you have worked out a time and date which will be suitable to all (or most) of those wishing to attend; some people may be travelling long distances and will appreciate a later start.

Telephone, or get someone else to telephone, the manager of the crematorium or cemetery. You will feel awkward about doing this but they will be used to private individuals contacting them: they'll know how to deal with your request.

Don't be nervous of stating your exact requirements – even better, ask for an appointment to visit to discuss the details: the procedure for the arrival, placing and removal of the coffin, music, seating arrangements, collection of ashes or preparation and filling in of the grave.

Carrying the coffin

Sealed coffins are twice as heavy as you think. It's most important that the bearers should be chosen more for their strength than from sentiment.

You will of course have checked (!), before putting the body in, that the coffin, when horizontal, can easily negotiate doorways, corridors and staircases.

Allow some time for the bearers to get used to the distribution of the weight before setting off. They will be using muscles they haven't used before.

The funeral gathering

> *I want everybody to have a good drink at my funeral and to cry. If they are not crying, I want them to pretend to cry – a load of them are supposed to be actors, for God's sake.*
>
> Oliver Reed, film actor

It's becoming commonplace for someone to leave a sum of money in their will to fund a get-together after the funeral. It's a sign of our ambivalence about these occasions that we are stuck for a name for them: a 'funeral tea' sounds old-fashioned, 'refreshments' sounds official and 'a party' is inappropriate.

They tend to become unplanned occasions that focus on a buffet and fizzle out after a couple of hours. It is, however, an important part of the function of a funeral – perhaps even the most important. It is the first act to take place after the body has been disposed of. It is a gathering of those people who were closest to the deceased where they can share their feelings and take stock of the future.

It makes a statement – 'This is what the world is like now she is gone.' It is a time for family and friends to regroup and is the first opportunity to begin to heal over the wound of loss. Like a wedding it serves the purpose of a family 'annual general meeting'.

Relationships are renewed, lesser conflicts can be resolved (or inflamed, sometimes) and the feeling of 'familyness' can be redefined.

The venue is important. First choice is usually the deceased's family home. However, this isn't necessary. Death often comes unexpectedly and the house might be in need of a spring clean or redecoration: it may be unfair on the surviving family for the relatives to have to be welcomed to the threadbare hall carpet and the peeling bathroom paint. This sounds a trivial matter but we all know how important such things can be.

Other family members will help get things ready, but it might be more comfortable for the gathering to take place somewhere else.

There are practical issues, as well. The tension of the funeral ceremony can be lessened by alcohol, but this needs to be balanced by the need for people to drive long distances afterwards. There are other tensions. Families these days often don't see much of each other and *there may be a good reason for this.* Life-long burning recriminations between relatives may also attend the gathering and the general atmosphere of open feelings can fan the flames.

Then there is the estate. Discretion will normally prevail but there will be curiosity about 'What's going to happen about his car?' or there may be whispering about the contents of the will. It's best to put off such things to a later date: this occasion should be about personal reminiscence, family updating and redefinition and, well done, it will make a sound basis for the bereavement to follow.

Home burials and cremations

Surprisingly, there is very little to stop you having a burial within your own property. It is unlikely, but check that there is nothing in the deeds of the property restricting burial.

The local authority planning department will tell you of any local by-laws – there may be a local regulation about the depth of the grave (often four feet of soil measured from the coffin lid).

You *may* need to get planning permission if what you are proposing amounts to a 'material change of use' – if you were thinking of burying more than one body for example – although another opinion is that you don't. The fact is that home burial is regarded as so 'unusual' and 'tasteless' by many people, courts and local authorities, laws and regulations are interpreted inconsistently.

One clear regulation is that any grave should be at least 40 feet away from any still or running water at, or close to, ground level, so you'll need a fairly large garden to get far enough away from the mains water supply.

There are other cautions about avoiding underground cables and pipework and a major safety issue about the actual spadework: digging a grave can be hazardous – keeping the sides and edges straight and firm is difficult. The geological make-up of the earth needs to be correct if it is not to collapse.

Perhaps the major consideration for most people will arise if they intend to move house in the future. Are you happy to pass over the ownership of the grave to strangers and will they be pleased to accept it? Will you tell them about it? Of course you would. If you didn't, what would happen when the new owners began to excavate their swimming pool?

It wouldn't be unknown for a householder to apply to the Home Office for an exhumation licence (£20) but would you want to take the body with you for reburial?

If you wish to proceed with a home burial, I strongly recommend that you buy a copy of the book *Green Burial, The D-I-Y Guide to Law and Practice* available from the Natural Death Centre, 20 Heber Road, London NW2 6AA. Tel: (020) 8208 2853. Fax: (020) 8452 6434. The author J. B. Bradfield is probably the foremost authority on the subject.

You can even cremate a body by yourself on your own property so long as you notify the Home Secretary of your 'intention to open a crematorium', you have all the certificates necessary for cremation and you have very, *very* understanding neighbours....

Woodland burials

For many people, the alternatives of conventional burial or cremation are not satisfactory. Cremation has associations of violence, unnecessary energy and pollution and cemeteries seem solemn, regimented and land-hungry. A woodland burial, however, far from destroying or 'warehousing' the body, allows someone to contribute to nature after their death.

There are now over 70 woodland burial sites in Britain run by a variety of organisations – farmers, local authorities, wildlife charities and private trusts or individuals.

After burial (in a biodegradable container) the ground is allowed to settle and a young tree is planted. Eventually, a wood will be created providing a habitat for birds and wildlife as well as a pleasant place to walk. A record is kept of all grave locations.

There is an Association of Nature Reserve Burial Grounds, which is proposing a code of practice that emphasises the protection of wildlife and the use of environmentally acceptable materials:

◆ The Association of Nature Reserve Burial Grounds, c/o The Natural Death Centre, 20 Heber Road, London NW2 6AA. Tel: (020) 8208 2853. Fax: (020) 8452 6434.

Organising a secular funeral

Less than half the weddings in Britain today take place in a church – and many of them involve people without a religious faith. When it comes to funerals, however, the vast majority include some sort of religious service.

It's a common experience for many people in the congregation to feel an unease about taking part in proceedings which imply sincere religious belief on their, and the deceased's, part. This is not surprising because the Christian funeral with which many people would have been familiar, based on the 1662 Prayer Book, was not about saying goodbye to a loved individual: it was intended as a stern farewell to a common sinner about to negotiate their future with their creator.

Nowadays, the form and content of more modern services may well reflect our wish to emphasise the past life of the dead person and to provide a quiet focus for people to come together to say goodbye. Nevertheless, a church setting can still invoke feelings of solemnity that may not chime with the mood of warmth and celebration that we may prefer. For people without a religious faith, churches often have an unintended oppressive feel about them.

Often the funeral ceremony is led by a duty minister who will perform several that day: it may be impersonal and contain inaccuracies. If you listen carefully as you leave the church you will hear murmured comments:

> *'He wasn't talking about Dad.*
> *'Aunty Jane never believed any of that.'*
> *'She made him sound like a saint.'*

On the other hand, using a lay officiant is no guarantee of success – some can be just as tedious, inaccurate or over-effusive, but humanistically.

However, in the confusion following a death, it's easy to 'just want to get through the funeral' and settle for a traditional religious service: it seems the easiest thing to do. To want to take an initiative and to do something different needs a strength and assurance that freshly bereaved people often lack.

Somewhere in the backs of our minds we also have the idea – we know it's wrong – that this sort of funeral is a 'requirement' and that there must be 'rules'. There aren't. You don't even need to have a ceremony at all.

However, it's generally accepted that there should be some sort of ceremony to mark someone's death. Just as a wedding is a public acknowledgement of an important stage in life – 'Things will be different from now on' – a funeral is a focus for a shared declaration that a life has ended. There is value in bringing together distant friends and relatives to mark the loss and reaffirm the family and community that remain.

The first step in organising a funeral ceremony should happen long before the death when everyone's wishes can be discussed. *Everyone* because, although we, as survivors, may want to arrange things the way the deceased person would have wanted, once they are dead we must feel comfortable with the ceremony and should not feel committed to something we will feel embarrassing or upsetting. There are four choices:

◆ a traditional religious service
◆ a secular ceremony with an officiant
◆ a ceremony involving family and friends
◆ no formal ceremony at all.

It may be that you want to have nothing to do with the details of the funeral. You may be so absorbed in grief that it is a kindness for a funeral director to take full responsibility for everything. You may or may not have discussed funeral arrangements earlier, but what you do now should be what feels best for you.

The easiest solution if you want a non-religious ceremony is to find someone to organise it. There is nothing to stop you asking a minister of religion to conduct a secular funeral. There may be objections from the Church to non-believers using the marriage service, but funerals are different. Ministers accept that they have a role to play in non-religious funerals for non-believers and will usually agree.

Unless the person who has died was an active member of a church, it is quite likely that the minister conducting a funeral, whether cremation or burial, will not have known him in person. A thorough briefing by a member of the family will help a skilled officiant to conduct the usual service in as personal a way as possible.

But for people with no particular religious faith, there may be an advantage in having the event conducted by someone who knew the dead person well, which is possible with a non-religious ceremony. This person could be a former colleague, family friend or relative.

You can arrange a secular ceremony by contacting the

British Humanist Association (BHA) who will put you in touch with a local 'officiant' (if there is one). He or she will contact the relevant family or friends and find out enough about the deceased to conduct a personalised ceremony, usually at a crematorium.

There are about 140 officiants accredited to the BHA. They come from a variety of backgrounds but each is carefully selected and undergoes a process of training and mentoring. There are equal numbers of men and women and each will perform an average of 24 ceremonies a year. (They sometimes also officiate at weddings.)

The ceremony will be short – crematoria are usually booked for 30 minutes. There will be an emphasis on celebrating the life of the deceased, recalling their beliefs and regretting their loss. There may be short readings or music but the officiant will tailor the ceremony to the wishes of the family. You can contact the British Humanist Association at:

◆ 30 Theobalds Road, London WC1X 8SP. Tel: (020) 8430 0908. Fax: (020) 8430 1271.
Email: robert@humanism.org.ukhttp.//
Website: www.humanism.org.uk

There will be a charge, usually paid through the funeral director. This will vary in different parts of the country but it should be similar to the fee charged by an Anglican minister for a funeral service (£60.00–£80.00).

The ceremony

It's worth giving some thought to the venue for the ceremony. Traditionally venues are churches, chapels and crematoria which are often sombre, restrained places. You might want to set a different tone.

Many people would say that the best funeral ceremonies are organised and conducted by the family and friends, if they can do it. They can speak with knowledge and experience and they can voice the feelings of those present.

There needs to be one person in overall charge of the proceedings and it's important that they can remain sufficiently in control to hold the shape of the ceremony together: it may be that those closest to the deceased should be excused this role.

However, maybe there is another family member with the simple organisational skill and confidence to take charge. There is no reason why it should not be a joint effort with others, but it does need co-ordination and planning:

- ◆ Who does what?
- ◆ Music?
- ◆ How are people received?
- ◆ Seating arrangements?
- ◆ Co-ordinating arrangements with the crematorium?
- ◆ Keeping strictly to time?

There are no rules about the content of the ceremony but usually two or three people will be able to put together a recital of reminiscences, anecdotes, appreciation, regrets, favourite readings and music.

What you say need not be long. It doesn't have to be an objective evaluation of someone's life, but it should be personal. Think of incidents that have happened to you or to others which give a sense of who the deceased was. There may have been peculiarities which irritated but which also defined them and endeared them to those around them.

Your remarks should be on the positive side of honesty: we want to remember the value they gave to the world. You don't have to say everything – but what you do say will almost certainly be appreciated more than an anodyne, vague and dishonest catalogue of bland remarks.

A most useful book to read is *Funerals Without God* by Jane Wynne Willson: this is published by the British Humanist Association (£5.00) (see page 168) but may be available in your local reference library. It has a suggested shape for the ceremony and a variety of 'script' examples for use in a variety of circumstances. Here's a flavour:

> *We are meeting here today to honour the life of Anne Smith*
> *and to bring consolation to those of her family and friends*
> *who are here.*
>> *Our ceremony will be a short and simple one, which will*

be in keeping with what she would have liked.

The world is a community, and Anne has been a part of that community. We are all involved in the life and death of each of us.

Human life is built on caring. It is natural that we should be sad today, because in a practical sense Anne is no longer part of our lives.

But we should not grieve – to live a good and fulfilling life for ninety years, with only the last year seriously marred by failing health, and then to die in one's sleep, is something to be thankful for.

Jayne Wynne Willson, *Funerals Without God*, 1989

Music

Choice of music is more personal nowadays: it can be a very powerful way of setting the right mood. We can be more imaginative in our choice these days, although wherever would we be without 'My Way'?

With the secularisation of death there is now an emphasis on looking back on a completed life rather than prayers for the future of the soul so, today, funeral music is often more about memories from the dead person's past.

Now that funerals are about celebration of a life as much as mourning of a death, Claire Rayner, agony aunt, points to the need for a peculiar blend of sorrow and laughter:

New Orleans Jazz is just perfect: wonderfully melancholic and uplifting. It leaves you feeling a little blue, so you're sad about losing the old bag, but it also makes you think, 'Wow, she was a bit of a cracker!'

It is this complexity of emotions that the traditional funeral music in the form of a simple lament is unable to address. Even Reverend Kenneth Lysens, who writes about hymns for the *Funeral Service Journal*, says:

Nothing is more depressing at a funeral than a doleful hymn, dolefully sung... Singability... is as important at funerals as it is at football matches.

Barbara Windsor sang 'The Boy I Love Is up In the Gallery' for Kenneth Williams. Brian Johnstone was played out of Westminster Abbey with 'Underneath the Arches'.

Barbara Smoker, President of the National Secular Society, who has officiated at funerals for 29 years, says that at the going-out all inhibitions are laid to rest.

The going-in needs to be a little sedate, but the going-out can be anything. I've had ballroom dancing and heavy metal.

Every year the Co-operative Funeral Service researches the top ten favourite pieces of music at funerals and cremations. This is the 1999 chart:

1. 'My Heart Will Go On' by Celine Dion
2. 'Candle in the Wind' by Elton John
3. 'Wind Beneath My Wings' by Bette Midler
4. 'Search For The Hero' by M-People
5. 'My Way' by Frank Sinatra
6. 'You'll Never Walk Alone' by Gerry and The Pacemakers
7. 'Release Me' by Engelbert Humperdinck
8. 'Memories' by Elaine Paige
9. 'Strangers In the Night' by Frank Sinatra
10. 'Bright Eyes' by Art Garfunkel

No ceremony

The fourth alternative is to have no formal ceremony at all. This might feel shocking but there can be circumstances when the whole business is just too painful for the family. A funeral ceremony is for their benefit after all: it should not be 'undergone' like a punishment. It will be a sad occasion inevitably but it should not be a negative experience.

The funeral could be delayed until feelings are not so raw. Alternatively, there could be an informal 'goodbye' get-together of family and friends from which the coffin could leave for the crematorium – maybe accompanied by one or two family members. However things are arranged, they should suit the needs of the bereaved survivors.

Because deaths and funerals are often sudden and very personal, families always have to start from scratch and reinvent the wheel. If we were better organised emotionally, socially and economically – we would organise ourselves into local co-operative societies where we could do the work for each other, as some religious groups do so successfully.

Write your own ceremony

Funeral ceremonies are usually conducted from the survivors' points of view – their memories of you and their sadness over their loss.

Why not take the initiative and leave a gift for your survivors – *your* ceremony celebrating your memories and appreciation of them? You are free to create your own format and content.

The only constraint may be time: a crematorium ceremony should normally last no more than 20 minutes to allow arrivals and departures within the 30-minute time slot.

You can write a 'script' for others to read or, more effectively, you could 'produce' a tape recording (or video) of your own, including text, music or other sounds. It's a strange experience to draft such a piece knowing the circumstances of its performance. However, you will find it an interesting and salutary task as it makes you consider what and whom you value in life.

It's not possible to provide a sample script as it will be the most personal piece you have ever written. However, the following phrases may prompt further thought:

- 'It is strange to talk with you in this way...'
- 'When I look back over my life...'
- 'I think of my childhood...'
- 'My parents...'
- 'I first met my husband/wife/partner...'
- 'Our early years together...'
- 'Of my friends...'
- 'My values and beliefs...'
- 'When I think of my children, they were each special in a different way...'

◆ 'My hopes for the future for my partner, children, family
and friends...'

It may seem hard to find the words at first – but in the end
you will have to cut out 75 per cent of the text to fit the
ceremony time. (However, don't throw the original away – put
it with your will.) Record it on a cassette tape, editing in music
if you want, and store the tape in a sealed envelope with your
will.

It may be wise to make two copies. Give one for
safekeeping to someone you can trust who is likely to survive
you. Keep a copy yourself: it may be many years before it is
needed and you may need to review what you have recorded,
and, if necessary, to do it again.

Write your own obituary

This could be incorporated into your will or be kept separate
for opening in the event of your death. It may be something
you could incorporate into your funeral service: your survivors
would appreciate such a last message.

On the other hand, you might feel too self-conscious to
actually write it down. There is no reason why you shouldn't
just ponder on the following statements which might help you
organise your thoughts and take stock of your life: there might
be something you could do to change things – there's still time.

◆ Other people would probably say that my main
achievements in life have been...
◆ For myself, what I am most pleased to have done with my
life is...
◆ If there is one thing I have learned in life it is...
◆ The three qualities I have tried to develop in my life are...
◆ The personal difficulties I have tried hardest to overcome
are...
◆ I have always wanted to see a world where...
◆ The people to whom I have felt closest are...
◆ Because...
◆ My greatest regret in life has been...
◆ If I had known how short a time I had left to live, I would
probably have...

Tape your own ceremony

You might consider using some of the material from a personal obituary as the basis for a funeral ceremony on tape. You could put together ten minutes of speech and music, which will serve to say 'goodbye' to the audience. Don't be greedy and use up all the time – others might want to say something about you.

All crematoria have facilities for replaying cassette tapes, but a portable cassette recorder would serve as well. You may need some discreet help to do the recording. You might even get someone else to produce a tape on your behalf – under your direction.

If I should die
and leave you
Be not like
others, quick
undone...
THOMAS GRAY

CHAPTER 8

After the Funeral Has Passed

*Y*ou cannot stop the birds of sorrow from flying over your
head,
But you can prevent them making nests in your hair.

Chinese proverb

Bereavement

This chapter relates to the loss of a close friend or partner.

Bereavement is usually described as though it were a large
black cloud of undefined but inevitable despair that falls on
someone following the death of a loved one: 'the greater the
love, the greater the grief'. It is unavoidable and only 'time' will
heal the hurt.

This is misleading and unhelpful. We all respond to
situations in different ways: there is no reason why the death of
a loved one should cause us all the same amount and quality of
personal hurt. How we react will depend upon the impact the
person has had on our lives, our own sense of ourselves and
how our previous life has prepared us to lessen the pain of
bereavement.

Until recent years it was considered 'brave' to face up to
bereavement with fortitude, but we're more grown up nowadays
and we're much more likely to acknowledge the hurt we feel in
our grief and the distress expressed by others in their
mourning. It is still common to hear 'She's taking it very well'
but most of us are aware of our need to express our feelings
and to be able to listen to the grief of others.

There is a danger, however, that in order to stress the
importance of the grieving process, we may be creating
'bereavement' as something separate, invariable and intense: a
defined process which must be carefully worked through and
assisted – preferably by someone who knows what they are
doing.

If you do not show the expected signs, you may be 'denying' your feelings. You're allowed a few months to work through the established sequence of 'stages' (not missing any out): there must be something wrong if you have not come to terms with the new situation and if you are not back to normal within 6–12 months. There is even an opinion that bereavement is a 'psychiatric disorder'.

I don't say that the pendulum has swung too far: that we have gone from neglect to over-emphasis. I don't wish to underestimate the feelings involved or the care we should offer to our grieving family and friends. The fact is that bereavement is much more complicated than popular psychology would have it and, oddly, the 'cure' for it, generally, is much more straightforward and matter-of-fact.

Elizabeth Kübler-Ross was a pioneer in modern attitudes to bereavement. She opened up the whole subject by describing the importance of the grieving process. She was the first person to describe it as more than being in a state of simple, but intense, sadness: she made us aware of the different components to grief and the care these demanded of others.

Unfortunately, in our enthusiasm for her ideas we were quick to latch on to her (I think unintended) teaching that there were a series of chronological 'stages' bereaved people should 'go through'. If they didn't follow this pattern they should be 'helped' to acknowledge it – because otherwise they would never successfully come to terms with their grief.

This has resulted in a general feeling that bereavement is 'serious': if you, as 'griever', don't go through these stages in the right order and with the correct intensity there is something the matter. As observers, we check out the griever's responses and worry about discrepancies. However, as we have always done, we continue to stand aloof because we don't feel qualified to tamper in such a 'serious' business.

Bereavement is not something special. It is simply loss. It may be catastrophic loss – greater than we have, or ever will, experience – but it is no more mysterious in the way that it affects us than any other loss.

One of the classic examples of the effects of loss is the blow to self-esteem and confidence that follow redundancy, dismissal or forced retirement from a valued job. Yet we all know of situations where what should have been a catastrophe was actually welcomed and turned out to be a positive experience, because the 'victim' was flexible enough to see alternatives. For someone else, an unplanned retirement could be disastrous: their job has provided the focus for their whole life – without it they are lost.

No two people, therefore, respond to a death in the same way. The nature of our grief will depend on:

◆ the attachment we have invested in the person lost
◆ our personal resources to make an alternative life.

Attachment

> *The distance that the dead have gone*
> *Does not at first appear.*
> *Their coming back seems possible*
> *For many an ardent year.*
>
> *And then, that we have followed them,*
> *We more than half suspect,*
> *So intimate have we become*
> *With their dear retrospect.*
>
> Emily Dickinson, 'The Distance that the Dead have Gone'

We cannot live a normal everyday life without *some* attachment. The roles we play in family and social life are fuelled by interdependence. We begin life totally dependent on others and we remain 'hooked' to our parents during childhood: we allow them to make decisions for us and we have few duties or responsibilities.

We get several opportunities to practise attachment and loss:

◆ We have to give up our exclusive attachment to our mother/father when we realise we've got to share them with her/his partner.
◆ Just as we're getting used to this, other babies might arrive and seem more successful than us at getting attention.
◆ Then, as we settle down to get on with life, we're uprooted from home and have to go to school. Here we have to learn new relationships: there are best friends, broken friendships

and dead guinea pigs to practise with.
- ◆ As adolescence arrives we find this dependence on home and school unhealthy, uncomfortable and unfair.
- ◆ We make a brave decision to unhook the ties and try out our independence (this is often – if not usually – done with a great deal of noise and fuss).

Parents have often become comfortable with their caring roles and do not like these ties being severed. How both parent and child handle this reluctant giving-up of dependence will be good practice for the way we handle later attachments.

There might be a couple of weeks in our early twenties when we are relatively attachment-free: we have created a social and emotional self-sufficiency. However, as we resume a more mature relationship with our families and develop deepening relationships with other people, we become drawn into a pattern of rewarding, positive attachments, which are likely to settle into long-term relationships.

It is here that roles and expectations become firmly established. We have probably selected our partner because of aspects of them that respond to needs within us: if these are mutually complementary it could be the start of a wonderful lifelong relationship. Most importantly, we may become exclusively dependent on each other for emotional and other supports. The stronger this partnership of mutual dependence is:

- ◆ the greater the anxiety each will have about dying first
- ◆ the harsher the blow for one when the other dies
- ◆ the more incapacitated the survivor will remain in the future.

This is all easy to understand. What is harder is to work out how we can improve the situation.

How to have closer relationships with reduced attachment

If I should die and leave you
Be not like others, quick undone,
Who keep long vigil by the silent dust and weep.

For my sake turn to life and smile....
Nerving thy heart and trembling hand
To comfort weaker souls than thee
Complete these unfinished tasks of mine
And I perchance may therein comfort thee.

Thomas Gray

The first thing to be said very clearly is that it is *not* necessary to reduce our commitment or closeness to those we love. However, we should avoid a situation developing by habit (or laziness) where we rely on partners and friends to live large parts of our lives for us. This can be starkly illustrated in the sort of family roles that have been common until recent years (and which still exist for many older people).

Men and women have traditionally made very different contributions to family life. Generally speaking, men have, in the past, been dependent on women for their home life, emotional support and family relationships and women have been dependent on men for earning money, decision-making and 'doing things'. Eventually our roles become hardened to exclude whole areas where we are dependent on the other person.

When either of the partners dies they take these parts of the other's life with them. Adjusting to the hurt caused is bereavement.

The way to lessen the pain then is to:

◆ Avoid putting all our emotional eggs into one relationship: make sure we maintain other friendships outside our immediate family – keep in touch with parents, other relatives and friends. If we spread our attachments the loss of one will not be devastating.

◆ Be familiar with all of the family tasks. Can we both: tune in a new video recorder, replace a zip, repair a broken windowpane, organise the family budget, operate the washing machine?

◆ Make sure that there are other positive interests in our lives than our relationship with our partner. 'She was his whole world' is a sad epitaph for a life-long relationship. 'So long as we've got each other' may sound warm and comforting, but it's a recipe for premature emotional decline for a surviving spouse.

Again, I should emphasise that this doesn't mean that we should avoid getting too close to our partner or that people ought not to have separate roles in a relationship. However, it's important to keep an eye on things so that we don't limit our flexibility, versatility, range of friendships and other interests – otherwise there will be tears before bedtime.

Fortunately these old-fashioned examples of family and gender roles are changing rapidly as men and women have begun to become more independent and share family roles and responsibilities.

> *The loss of my husband was inconvenient and expensive. I never realised until he had gone just how many small jobs he did around the house. A toilet-roll holder that has pulled loose from the wall, Stanley would have plugged and reset. Now I have to try to do it myself, or find a handyman and pay him.*
>
> *Sometimes there are two or three trivial chores I cannot do myself, and they snowball together into a major, daunting problem ... I very badly wanted a man – not in the usually debased sense of the phrase. I wanted a strong, male presence. Something deep inside me, something that makes me feminine, makes me a woman, needed masculinity – a mirror in which I could reflect and so find myself. Without this I was formless, nothing ... A part of me, so basic I had never discovered it before, needed masculinity so that I could remould myself against it. . . .*
>
> *People said, 'I'm so sorry to hear you've lost your husband,' but what no one seemed to realise was that I had lost myself. And that was much more serious.*
>
> Mary Jones, *Secret Flowers*

> *Spouses have to be able, ideally, to accept the idea that 'their' person can and will, if necessary, go on without them, and even find new resources in the experience. You need also to accept that you yourself can, and will if necessary, go on without your partner and find resources there too. This does not preclude grief at loss, gratitude for what has been and*

loyalty to a relationship now discharged to the full...

If these things are, indeed, faced (and the relationship is deepened by facing them) bereavement is not painless – grief will and should be felt and expressed. But it will lack the elements of guilt, self-deception and role-playing which contribute far more than genuine love to making bereavement destructive to the survivor.

Alex Comfort, A Good Age, Mitchell Beazley 1977

We find major losses difficult to deal with and we will fight hard to prevent the disruption of our lives. When we lose a partner or other family member to whom we are closely attached, we still fight against the loss instinctively.

The most difficult losses to bear are those which:

◆ require us fundamentally to review our way of living
◆ are not just temporary, but permanent
◆ happen suddenly, without preparation, and require immediate change.

The physical damage that grief can cause

We've looked earlier at the part that stress can play in our lives. We tend to think of bereavement as a time of quiet feelings of loss and sadness, but underlying this the ravages of stress are at work.

We are faced with catastrophe and our 'fight or flight' impulse comes into play. This has the physiological effect of mobilising our body for immediate action but there is no one to fight and nowhere to run. Our body, however, remains poised for action, diverting resources from other – inessential for the moment – parts. Thus deprived, the performance of our brains, hearts, digestive and reproductive systems is reduced and their inefficiency soon begins to show.

Appetite may alter, sleep might be disturbed. There may be palpitations and chest pains, the bladder and menstruation might be affected. We might feel dizzy and confused – this might be increased by anti-depressants.

The quickest way to relieve stress is to exercise. It seems inappropriate to encourage someone in the midst of bereavement to go swimming or cycling, but if they were able to take some vigorous exercise some of the background stress could be relieved.

Less commonly, people react to a death by shutting down completely: it is as though their whole system has 'fused' in the face of massive emotional overload. They might be flat and unresponsive, apparently unaware of their surroundings or what has happened. They will gradually adjust to the situation, helped by quiet, unfussy support.

Mostly these physical effects are temporary and we recover. Whilst there is little evidence that an important loss can lead generally to increased mortality in the survivor, there is some evidence that – especially among older widowers – severe grief can lead to increased cardio-vascular disease and premature death.

There is also an underrated risk that depression, which is not dramatically evident, can continue and can grow imperceptibly to become a chronic, untreated, lifelong disability.

It's not, however, all doom and gloom

> *Death has got something to be said for it;*
> *There's no need to get out of bed for it:*
> *Wherever you may be,*
> *They bring it to you, free.*

Kingsley Amis

There is a fallacy that bereavement is inevitably a time of overwhelming distress and that it is essential to be able to show the depth of our grief closely following the death.

There have been several American studies which reveal that between 25 per cent and 65 per cent of widows and widowers were 'not greatly distressed' by their loss. In a review of this research, Dr Camille Wortman, a Michigan University psychologist, said that the lack of deep distress:

> *can be a sign of resilience. Many have worldviews – often a*
> *spiritual outlook – that lets them see the loss in a way they*
> *can accept.*

There is an old puritan belief in some religious groups, which frowns on emotional outbursts and which encourages the belief that the dead person has passed to a more exalted existence. Extreme grief in these circumstances may be viewed as an indulgence. This is not the denial and unwillingness to face reality that we sometimes see, but a genuine – enviable to some of us – way of making sense of things.

> *If I should go before the rest of you*
> *Break not a flower nor inscribe a stone*
> *Nor when I'm gone speak in a Sunday voice*
> *But be the usual selves that I have known.*
> *Weep if you must, parting is hell,*
> *But life goes on,*
> *So sing as well.*
>
> Joyce Grenfell, *Joyce: By Herself and her Friends*

> *If one of us were to die, I think I might get some new curtains*
> *for the living room.*
>
> Quoted by Freud

How to be bereaved successfully

Sit down on your own for an hour and think about your family and your friends. Go through them one by one and imagine what their response would be to your death. It would be unusual if you were not missed and the cause of sadness. But who might be devastated? And why?

The chances are that the person to take it hardest – a partner perhaps – will be someone with whom you have a close but (like all of us) imperfect relationship.

We can read about perfect relationships in books. These are partnerships where both people unreservedly accept each other and share an unconditional love. There are no games or rivalries: no lies or deceptions. Even the happiest of real relationships is not immune from misunderstandings, impatience, irritability and manipulations.

The more we complicate things by hiding true feelings, exercising power or having secrets from each other, the greater will be our partner's difficulty in adjusting to our loss: we will have confused them about what they are losing.

The remorse — and who has not felt it after a death — was worse; the most unpleasant thing I have ever experienced. I was attacked by memory. I realised how often I must have wounded his feelings, and I now realised how the hurt had been done casually and unconsciously; my indifference and self-absorption: my lack of understanding and petty resentments. I was often hard, antagonistic and unforgiving.

Mary Jones, *Secret Flowers*

Although the perfect partnership doesn't exist, there is nothing to stop us working towards it. This mainly means being open, sorting out differences and above all being careful about any dominating or submissive aspects that might creep into the relationship: a shared, positive equality in which each values the other should be our aim.

When we die we should be 'fully known' by our partner: we should not leave any skeletons in the cupboard, undisclosed mistresses at the funeral, pornography in the garage, undeclared overdrafts or other nasty surprises.

If, as the bereaved person, we have mixed feelings of fear, anger or resentment about our partner, they tend to remain bottled up and unexpressed. When they die we no longer have the opportunity to confront these feelings: to talk to other family members about them would be embarrassing and disloyal.

In circumstances like these, when we have confused and distressing feelings, it might be useful to seek out a friend or counsellor to talk to outside the close family.

From the above you will see that the nature of our grieving will have been laid down long before the death which occasioned it. If we wish not only to anticipate our own response to bereavement but also to ease our own loss for others, we may need to alter our attitudes and behaviour now.

Ask yourself about your own death. Would you want the people you leave behind to be perpetually miserable, and you to have caused that misery by your death? If we are honest about it, most of us will admit to wanting people to be sad that we have died, but we also want them to be glad they knew us, and to be happier in some way as a result of our life.

We would not want them to be forever miserable because of us when we are dead. And we also need to ask whether it is really possible for the death of somebody near to us to be the sole cause of our being forever unhappy.

If we spend the rest of our life being miserable, surely a part of the responsibility for that reaction must be our own. How can we blame it on the death of that person? To say that another person's death has caused this is ultimately no different from blaming that person for causing our unhappiness by dying.

Dr Tony Lake, *The Tasks of Grieving*

The more subtle injuries of grief

Bereavement will leave us preoccupied with our sadness and bewildered about the future. While this takes our attention we may not notice other effects of the loss which could become even more harmful.

All our emotional and psychological energy is focused on our crisis. It is only when we have such a massive distraction like this that we realise how much we take for granted our normal shrewdness and intelligence about day-to-day living:

◆ We might lose our usual restraint about impulsive decisions: 'Ring the estate agents – this place has too many sad memories for me.'

◆ Our stagnant emotional condition may drive us to seek dangerous physical sensations – spending money, giving things away, an ill-advised, comfort-seeking sexual adventure.

◆ We may become regrettably uninhibited: 'It was the job with your company and your f****** bullying that killed him!'

◆ We might be drawn into the long-term damage of anaesthetics – alcohol or anti-depressants.

When we are in the throes of early grief we may be in no fit state to make decisions or look after our long-term interests. We may need someone to be with us – with the impossible task of closely supervising us and, at the same time, allowing us to feel free to express feelings and remain in charge of our lives.

We may in particular need someone to be close, particularly if we are looking after children: we are temporarily disqualified from a caring role – especially of people who have serious grief needs of their own.

After some months, when the tears are less, we might think that *now* is the time to pull ourselves together and 'move on'. In a way this is an even more dangerous notion because decisions may seem 'reasonable' and friends will be less willing to interfere – but we may be just as wrong. We may get ideas into our heads, which are wholly erroneous and disabling – but they are very sticky and may harden into long-term resolutions:

◆ 'It would be disloyal for me to look for another relationship.'

◆ 'I'm useless now without his support: no one could ever replace him.'

There's no reason why we shouldn't be able to confront such weasel notions on our own, but we'll be better served by the support of a close friend who can steer us back to emotional and practical reality.

Be careful of your friends though ....

Whilst, previously, our identity was the business of only us and our partner, after their death we might become vulnerable to interference from others. They may wish to impose their own ideas of who we should be and what we should be doing:

◆ In their eyes we may be a tragic victim needing careful handling.

◆ We may be seen as a deprived sexual creature needing 'comfort'.

◆ We may be seen as suddenly rich and 'eligible'.

◆ Others might see us as a threat to their marriages.

However we are regarded, because of our vulnerability, we may not be able to understand these 'odd' attitudes and we'll need to guard against misunderstandings and well-meant but offensive confrontations.

Grief opportunities

To suggest that there can be a positive side to grief is at first rather shocking. However, we must face the fact that the loss of an important relationship not only removes that person from us but, in time, provides us with the opportunity of reassessing our life and a freedom to develop in new ways.

We have seen earlier that the pleasures of attachment to someone are usually achieved by making compromises – we may give up some of our personal hopes and ambitions, quite reasonably, for the (more important) success of the relationship.

We can now choose either:

◆ to regret and mourn these 'sacrifices' that have been 'wasted'

◆ or to be thankful for the relationship – now lost – and, after a while, take stock of our personal resources and resurrected aspirations and review the new possible pathways into the future.

The other, more general, 'opportunity' of bereavement is the way that we gain a more mature understanding of the meaning of relationships. In addition:

◆ We can gain a fuller, more mature perspective on life and cherish our other relationships more realistically.

◆ We can refocus our life and imagine how *we* can achieve a 'good death'. We may be more open with our feelings.

◆ We have had an insight into loss, which will enable us to empathise with other people in their grief.

Helping bereaved people

> *There's a newspaper report of a (primary) school in New York where, following the death of the class hamster, a team of bereavement counsellors were hired.*
> Talk Radio, December 1998

Most people are nervous of dealing with strong negative emotions in other people – and we fear that some bereavement feelings can be very 'dangerous'.

We are aware of 'bereavement counselling' and we are more educated than ever to consider grief as being a complex

condition requiring sensitivity that hints at specially acquired
skills. This discourages us from seeing ourselves as having an
important part to play in helping someone's bereavement:

◆ 'I wouldn't know what to say.'
◆ 'I'm frightened of saying the wrong thing.'
◆ 'He needs proper help.'
◆ 'I'm worried she might do something silly.'

We've picked up that 'helping' involves someone with a
problem coming to someone with greater knowledge or
experience for a solution: whatever it means, we can be
forgiven for thinking that 'helping' means 'doing something' –
and using special skills:

> One of the most distressing things was the behaviour of my
> neighbour: we used to be very friendly, meeting regularly and
> sharing family problems. When Philip died she stopped coming
> round. If we saw each other in the garden she would ask me
> how I was – but making it very clear that the answer she
> wanted was, 'Just fine'.
>
> Margery Lambert

There are times when we come across situations in life which
overwhelm us, when we are fearful that we are out of our
depth and we can only recover with help – skilled help.
Bereavement is rarely such a time. If we are grieving the last
sort of help we need is someone to assess and analyse our
behaviour and to give us knowing advice about how we can
make our grief go away.

We need someone who will 'be' with us and keep a channel
open to our feelings. It is not at all a simple process but
successful mourning seems to involve us in:

◆ fully recognising and acknowledging our pain
◆ translating the raw feelings into accurate words
◆ transmitting the description to someone else
◆ someone else 'hearing' the expressed feelings
◆ the 'someone else' showing the griever that the feelings have
  been correctly understood.

Just why it is that there is some healing magic in this communication exchange is unclear: it's as though the pain is reduced when the feelings are described to, and acknowledged by, someone else.

Tears produce a similar effect: the pain seems capable of being liquefied in the tear ducts and expressed through the eyes. It's hard to know why we cry so effectively, but we do.

It is important to realise that there is no need to make suggestions or give advice. The main qualification is a genuine unselfish willingness to give our time and attention; most mature adults can do this. Often 'experts' make a mess of it – their professional 'responsibility' can interfere with the simple humanity required.

Because there is no responsibility on us to 'guide' conversation, we can take pauses – even long ones – in our stride. We should allow the style and pace of conversation to be set by the person doing the grieving.

We should also prevent our own experiences from intruding. We may genuinely think that to hear about our 'even more tragic' bereavement last year will help bring some hope and proportion to the situation. However, our experiences, although relevant, can come across as irrelevant and disabling.

We should not underestimate the practical help we can give – shopping, cooking, looking after pets or answering the telephone.

If we don't feel able to visit or talk to the griever, we can write a letter. The following is from a piece by Virginia Ironside in *The Times* (29 July 1992) describing how comforting it was to receive letters after her father's death:

> *I will never let another death go by without dropping the relatives a line. Letters that say things like 'He will live on forever in your heart' – trite lines I'd usually wrinkle a lip at – seem to have huge significance, laden with meaning. 'I am down the road if you want an ear' came from an old schoolfriend I barely knew.*
>
> *And a lovely line from my son's godfather. 'These sad deaths are like signposts which direct you into a new and unknown route. I can only wish you well.'*

We have had testimonies from journalists and other public figures who have written about their confrontation with death – Derek Jarman, Harold Brodkey, Dennis Potter, Jill Tweedie, Ruth Picardie, John Diamond – it's a new development: discussion about dying is becoming part of our social agenda.

We're actually beginning to be able to joke about it. Marti Caine, the comedian, was asked whether her cancer had changed her attitude to life. Her reply:

> *You start by watching the daffodils and end up watching 'Neighbours'.*

*I know death
hath ten
thousand
several doors for
men to take
their exit.'*
JOHN WEBSTER

CHAPTER 9

Different Deaths

W e tend to think that the death of a spouse is the hardest
loss we shall have to bear. We have so much of
ourselves invested in our partners that the losses for us are
immediately apparent and dramatic. However, other deaths can
be just as devastating.

The death of a parent

> *One reason you are stricken when your parents die is that the
> audience you've been aiming at all your life – shocking it,
> pleasing it – has suddenly left the theatre.*
>
> Katherine Whitehorn, *The Observer* 1983

We have always expected that our parents will die before us
and usually there are few obvious ties of dependence left for
their deaths to have an obvious impact on the structure of our
lives. This is often deceptive.

Our relationship with our parents stands discreetly in the
background of our lives; we never had to choose them, there
was an inevitable bonding and we didn't have to 'work' at the
relationship to keep it going. Because it was 'just there' we
usually took it for granted more than we should. As we grow
into adulthood we transfer our dependence on our parents to a
commitment to a partner and family. Because we are so
preoccupied with establishing this family and home of our own,
the 'presence' of our parents recedes.

However, we should not underestimate the significance of
their deaths. They have been, for all our childhoods, the most
important people in the world. Even if we have been unhappy
or abused, we cannot escape the impact they had on us and
which they continue to have. We can never be indifferent.

When they die, therefore, there will be an inevitable effect on us. Even if we have become totally independent and they have become reliant on us, they will never have lost their function as an 'anchor' in our lives – the 'home-base' to which we unconsciously relate everything that ever happens to us.

We rarely put this relationship into words, we may rarely see them from one month to another, but when we lose them, something important happens to us: the bonds are destroyed. Mainly we have valued these bonds: their unconditional love, their wisdom, a place where we're always welcome.

Sometimes we will guiltily be pleased to be free of aspects of their influence that we have resented since childhood: their criticism, their interference, their domination.

Usually we will have mixed feelings.

We sometimes find it difficult to share feelings with our partners but this is even truer of parent–child relationships. This is not surprising considering the potential for difficulties as a child grows from total dependency to adulthood: all sorts of resentments, jealousies and rivalries mingle with love, comfort and protection. We find it hard to put our feelings for our parents into words – so we remain silent. Yet there is usually a yearning to keep up a closeness and intimacy with them.

Because of the arrogance of youth and our need to assert our own separate identity, we usually treat our parents badly – but we're reticent to talk about our feelings with them. Unless we somehow 'make our peace' and allow them to appreciate our positive feelings for them before they die, we are left with regrets that can never be made good.

It's important for them and for us that we communicate the best of our feelings with them. We can do this directly or – just as good – through our actions and behaviour: keeping in regular touch, being available, a simple hug.

Other people aren't so sensitive to this sort of loss – people who have lost their parents are not given the attention by others that a new widow or widower will get. Because of the entanglement of family relationships it may be easier for a bereaved son or daughter to talk about how they feel to someone outside the family:

*It was a terrible time: everybody was at sixes and sevens after
(my father) died – it was just not appropriate to talk to them,
they were so upset.*

*One day I got talking to someone at work – we weren't
even friends particularly. He'd never known my father so I
didn't feel the need to be careful what I said. It was easy
talking to him and I said things to him that I had never
actually put into words for myself before. He was able to help
me see that Dad probably did know how much I cared.*

Phil Jenkins

The death of a child

*She was in form and intellect most exquisite. The unfortunate
parents ventured their all on this frail bark and the wreck was
total.*

Eighteenth-century gravestone of nine-year-old Penelope Boothby

*His laughter was better than birds in the morning, his smile
Turned the edge of the wind, his memory
Disarms death and charms the surly grave.
Early he went to bed, too early we
Saw his light put out; yet we could not grieve
More than a little while,
For he lives in the earth around us, laughs from the sky.*

C. Day Lewis

Although we have had a lifetime to prepare for the death of
our parents, we, as parents, can rarely be prepared for the
death of our child. It is 'against nature' that a child should die
before being allowed to contribute its genes to the next
generation: it has 'failed' genetically and so have we: there have
been 'wasted' years of hope and expectations: it seems cruel.

It is cruel. There is a cruel, genetic 'correctness' that an
'unfit' bundle of genes should not be permitted reproduction.
But that's no comfort to anyone. When one of our children
dies it seems the most serious thing that can happen to us. Our
purpose for being here has come to nothing.

When an older person dies there is normal personal
grieving but, after the immediate shock of the loss of a child,

our first response is to challenge the circumstances – such is the 'unnatural', incredible impact of the event.

Compare it to a rail incident: coaches get derailed, a locomotive over-runs the buffers, somebody falls on the line from an insecure door. These are all serious matters and regrettable but we take them in our stride – it's normal for accidents to happen. However, when you get a head-on collision causing multiple casualties, this isn't normal – we demand a public enquiry.

So it is with the death of a child: we will leave no stone unturned until we have made some sense of the circumstances. Something terrible must have gone wrong to bring about such a monstrous biological mistake: we must do something to see that 'it'll never happen again to someone else.' This desire for investigation and need for action can become the driving force for lengthy litigation: it can be the basis for a campaign – the beginning of a pressure group or a charity.

There is a need to 'achieve' something on behalf of the child – almost to make up for the 'lost achievements' of the son or daughter: 'so that, at least, something good can come out of this...'.

The energy and tenacity of our will to understand can have a strange effect. Normal social reserve becomes irrelevant: we have lost 'everything', there is nothing worse that can happen to us. Normal inhibitions are loosened and we can develop a previously unseen confidence and verbal skill that may make us appear provocative and 'dangerous'.

It's possible for one or both parents to become stuck in this 'active' mode for some time, spending a fortune, travelling, organising petitions, writing to the papers, reading law books. There are parents, for example, whose children were murdered decades ago, whose shock and anger are as fresh today as the day it happened.

In the short term, this 'busyness' can be helpful as an anaesthetic for the intolerable pain inside and it can mask some of the quieter feelings of bereavement, but these will surely come – the depression, the guilt, the 'if onlys'.

When an older person dies, it is in the order of things: they may have raised a family, their faculties may have been beginning to fade – their life is 'behind' them. When a child dies, however, they have still to 'blossom' into maturity. As a parent, we will have been looking forward to their future beside them: we will have seen the promise of musical or sporting achievement, the rudiments of a maternal instinct, the aptitude for mathematics.

It is hard to set aside these hopes and aspirations: with the loss of a child it is much more difficult to close down our imagination for the future. We will remember their birthday for the rest of our lives: 'she would have been 33 yesterday.' A part of them will always live:

> *The first time one man and his wife were asked at a dinner party how many children they had was only a few months after their son had died. The father says:*
>
> *'I knew R. (his wife) couldn't answer. But I knew if I told the truth, if I said: "Well, we did have three children, but one died", I wouldn't get through the sentence. And I didn't want to upset the host and his wife either, who were close friends. So, in the end, I said. "Two." And as soon as I said it I knew what a mistake it was. If felt as if I had denied my son his life, and I said there and then I would never do it again.'*
>
> Carol Lee, *Good Grief*, Fourth Estate 1994

When we grieve for an adult we can conceive of eventual normality – 'it's been sad, but that's life'. After the loss of a child, however, things will never be the same again: part of us will have been permanently harmed. We'll learn to live with the wound, but it will never heal.

Although this book is about preparing for death, it is not productive to anticipate the death of our children beyond normal safety measures. To be overprotective and to dwell on the possibility of disaster is against the whole spirit of hope and growth that should be part of family life. There is a sense in which children can only make the leap into maturity by our encouragement of a reckless (but sensible) disregard for their mortality.

This is not to say that we should pass on 'death-denying' attitudes to our children. We can let them know about the reality of birth, reproduction and death in the context of a wonderful, integrated 'life story' rather than separating death off as the dreadful enemy.

We know, after all, the damage that the world did to us when it told us about death.

> *Some people are bound to die young. By dying young a person*
> *stays young forever in people's memories. If he burns brightly*
> *before he dies, his light shines for all time.*
>
> Alexander Solzhenitsyn

Miscarriage, stillbirth and baby death

To lose a young, developing child is hard, but even a young child will have had a characteristic personality – a presence and individuality that was evident to family and friends and the loss of which can be shared.

The miscarried or stillborn child, however, will have a socially 'unknown' identity and will not have 'existed' so tangibly for others as for the parents – especially the mother. Even the parents will have very little to 'remember' about its unlived life.

As prospective parents we build up a 'fantasy' baby in our minds in which we invest our hopes, dreams and expectations: if the baby doesn't survive, part of ourselves is also 'lost'.

A study in 1990 estimated that clinically recognised miscarriages occur in up to 31 per cent of pregnancies. Because of this frequency, the non-visibility of the foetus and the assumption that there is no parent/child relationship, the effects are underestimated: yet there are no significant differences between the grief responses of women losing their babies through miscarriage, stillbirth or neonatal death.

> *Assumption of 'no grief' following miscarriage may be little*
> *more than an admission of ignorance, because no one follows*
> *up this mother to find out how she does or does not recover.*
>
> Rosemary Mander, *Loss and Bereavement in Childbearing*,
> Blackwell 1994

The assumption that there is little relationship between parents and foetus is challenged by the use of ultra-sound scanning of the womb which allows parents to see – and bond – with their child at *six weeks* in a way that was only possible at 20 weeks a generation ago.

There are other special, often unrecognised, problems about dealing with the death of a baby:

◆ Often the mother is young – without the maturity to come to terms with loss. This may be her first experience of death.

◆ Childbirth is to do with 'health', growth and hope: a baby's death is always shocking, particularly if the mother's antenatal care had given her 'a clean bill of health'.

◆ The mother may suffer an overwhelming sense of guilt: did she do something wrong? Was she unfit to bear children?

◆ Because of the intimacy of pregnancy the mother has a unique relationship with her unborn baby – much more 'bonded' and special than was previously thought. She 'knows' her baby in a way that no one else can – her loss, in this sense, is a lonely one.

◆ Those around her, whilst shocked and distressed, will have a lesser experience of the loss than the mother and may underestimate the care she needs.

◆ Whilst the need for grieving may be underestimated in the mother, it is commonly totally overlooked in the father. His greater reticence to express his feelings may leave his bereavement completely ignored. He may set aside his grief needs to support the mother.

Miscarriage, stillbirth and neonatal death are unwanted tragedies, but similar grief responses happen even when the loss is sought – as in pregnancy termination because of foetal abnormality or for other reasons. The effect can be much more complex than that of 'relief': there may be feelings of inadequacy, self-recrimination and guilt.

Suicide

◆ About 5,000 people commit suicide in the United Kingdom every year.

◆ At least 200,000 people attempt suicide every year.

◆ In the 15–19 age group, 750 people in every 100,000 attempt suicide – more than twice as many as ten years ago.

- ◆ Suicide attempts and successful suicides are increasing faster for young people than any other age group.
- ◆ Suicide is the third most important cause of death for young people.
- ◆ Someone who has previously attempted suicide is more than 1,000 times as likely to try again than someone who has not.

When assessing the risk of someone taking their own life, doctors and other professionals have a checklist of high risk predisposing factors:

◆ male	◆ 15–25 years
◆ over 65 years	◆ white
◆ divorced	◆ widowed
◆ unemployed	◆ retired
◆ poor health	◆ living alone
◆ previous attempt	◆ previous threats
◆ fantasises of violent methods	◆ spring or summertime

The occupations at the greatest risk are:

◆ doctors	◆ vets
◆ pharmacists	◆ dentists
◆ sailors	◆ farmers
◆ forestry workers	◆ students
◆ prisoners	

The British geography of suicide

Within England and Wales there is a wide variation in the incidence of suicide according to local authority areas. The highest rates are in areas where high deprivation is measured by such factors as unemployment, one-parent families and chronic illness. The Pennine area is especially noteworthy.

In Manchester, in particular, where it is estimated that 10 per cent of men are clinically depressed, a recent survey revealed that there were 208 suicides per 100,000 of the population among men between 15 and 44 years of age – 1.7 times more than the average. The female rate was 2.3 times higher than the average. This compares with an amazing figure of 4 young male suicides per 100,000 population during the same period in South Herefordshire. Similarly low figures are typical of other prosperous areas in the Home Counties and 'growth' areas in south and central England.

> *Curious fact. Suicide is responsible for the deaths of one in four Chinese women: worldwide, 56 per cent of all women who commit suicide are Chinese. Nobody knows why.*
>
> Reported in *When we Die*, Cedric Mims, 1998

'It was all my fault'

When someone close to us takes their own life they are using their death as the ultimate message of despair. It is easy to think of it as an aggressive act but that is to undervalue the person's distress and self-absorption and to exaggerate our own responsibility.

However, we will feel some responsibility. If we were caught up in the person's life before they died, we can imagine how we might have contributed – the unreturned telephone call, the unintended snub, all that remained unsaid.

Perhaps it isn't just fantasy. What if we were responsible: we caused them to kill themselves? It can never be as clear as that. What was it in the sum of their life experiences that predisposed them to respond to us at this time in this sad way? You are permitted guilt only if you seriously intended them to take their life. However, if we were close to the person we will not escape the suspicion that there may have been something we could have done to change the outcome:

- 'If only we'd had another baby....'
- 'If only I hadn't left home....'
- 'If only we'd managed to keep up the mortgage....'

Forget it: the 'might-have-beens' of life are the first steps to madness. As we recover from the shock we will realise that we can learn more profitably to pay more attention to the 'what-ifs?' of the future.

One unfortunate aspect of bereavement following suicide is that research has shown that there may be ill-feeling from others towards us: there may be some disquiet, similar to our own, that we must have contributed to the death in some way.

There's nothing we can do about this except to be more alert
in the future to others' needs who might be in our situation.

(The good news, reported in *The Observer* (16 May 1999) is
that the Treasury has published 600 efficiency and performance
aims. One target is for suicides to be reduced by 17 per cent by
2010. So that's all right then.)

> *There are many who dare not kill themselves for fear of what
> the neighbours might say.*
>
> Cyril Connolly, *The Unquiet Grave*, 1944

Death in other cultures,

> *A soldier going to place flowers on the grave of a fallen
> comrade met a native (sic) carrying a food-offering to his
> ancestral tomb. Amused by this superstitious absurdity, the
> soldier asked him when his ancestors would emerge from the
> tomb to enjoy their meal.*
>
> *'About the same time as your friend comes up to smell your
> flowers,' he answered.*
>
> Puckle, *Funeral Customs*, 1926

The traditions associated with death in our European-American
culture have been shaped by Christian ideas and practices.
These tend to be restrained – solemn even. Funerals are quiet,
short affairs – a tear might be shed but feelings usually remain
private.

We have much to learn from other cultures that mostly give
greater visible significance to a death. Dying often has a deeper
meaning for those who remain and rituals are much more
established, lengthy and elaborate. The upheaval in family
relationships is noted and changed roles are acknowledged.

The expression of grief can vary from the shrieking distress
of a Hindu family to the gentler acceptance of bereaved
Buddhists – both an authentic expression of a shared, profound
belief in the meaning of death. Maybe our British confusion
and reticence about death is a similar (sad?) reflection of our
lack of shared spiritual belief.

In other cultures the process of dying, preparing and
disposing of the body, mourning and bereavement are linked

to very specific practices: these make the process of dealing with death a very active one which engages people in particular ways. The process has a visibility and presence that often seems much healthier than our hushed tones and respectful silences.

On the other hand, our 'respectability' and our inhibitions about expressing feelings or religious rituals may make us horrified at some of the extreme emotions and physical arrangements for the body: we may not understand different attitudes to bereavement. This may lead to discrimination against people from other ethnic traditions who need to use British health services, mortuaries, Coroners, cemeteries and crematoria.

It's intriguing that cultures which have clearly agreed, shared rituals about grief and mourning have an almost complete absence of 'prolonged grief'.

Death and homosexuality

If a dying person is homosexual and in a long-term relationship, there may well be strains on family relationships. In the past it was sadly common for parents to reject the homosexuality in their children and there is sometimes an unspoken estrangement from them.

There is often a dilemma that arises here, because if their child develops a terminal illness the parents will often wish to care for them – thus excluding the partner and friends. There is not enough time in the final months and weeks for them to shed a lifetime of prejudice and there is a risk of tense recriminations from all parties at a time when there needs to be warmth and unity.

The dying person will almost certainly want their partner, friends and family to be at peace with each other; it is unforgivable that hostility should be other than suppressed by everyone at this time.

This does not mean that feelings should not be expressed. Indeed, to be able to attempt to get to know and understand each other's feelings will go a long way towards any desired reconciliation.

It may be that the person is dying in their own home, being cared for by a long-term partner. In the heterosexual equivalent relationship, the spouse would normally have the principal role in decision-making, consents, funeral arrangements and executing a will. Their right as next of kin and beneficiary are established even if there is no will.

Homosexual partners, however, have no legal status. If they were financially dependent on the deceased they could make a claim if there was no will, but they otherwise have no rights.

This makes it essential that both partners have drawn up wills that make their wishes clear. There should also be agreement by everyone about funeral arrangements – who will organise it and who will attend.

Further information can be obtained from:

◆ The Terrence Higgins Trust, 52–54 Gray's Inn Road, London WC1X 8JU. Tel: (020) 7831 0330.

◆ Gay Bereavement Project, Unitarian Rooms, Hoop Lane, London NW1. Tel: (020) 8455 8894.

HIV/AIDS and death

Life expectancy of babies born in Zimbabwe five years ago.
61 years
Life expectancy this year due to the prevalence of HIV/AIDS.
39 years

Independent on Sunday, November 1998

AIDS is now (1999) the world's leading infectious killer, causing six million deaths a year. It is a more common cause of death than tuberculosis, diarrhoea or lung infections and is only exceeded by strokes, heart and pulmonary disease.

In the autumn of 1998 there were 33.4 million people who had been diagnosed as HIV positive and the number is rising by about 16,000 a day: over 13 million people have died since the epidemic began. Seventy per cent of these new diagnoses are in African cities and of these 10 per cent are women. At one point people were dying at the rate of one every twelve minutes.

In the United Kingdom during the last 14 years, there have been 32,000 HIV positive diagnoses, 11,000 have died and 4,500 people are presently significantly ill. The emphasis has shifted from homosexual men to heterosexual partners: of these (6,665 diagnosed at the end of 1998) more than half are women.

There is a 12–30 per cent chance that a woman can pass the HIV virus on to her unborn child. It is hard to be sure if this has happened until the child is tested at 18 months: until then a positive result could just show that the baby has their mother's antibodies.

Because of effective health education, the incidence of HIV/AIDS in Britain is significantly lower than in France, Portugal, Spain and Italy.

The concern now is for Africa and other developing countries where there is less public awareness and no money for medication. In sub-Sahara East Africa it is estimated that 10 per cent of the rural population is infected and in many cities 35 per cent of women of child-bearing age are HIV positive – mostly undiagnosed.

There are sometimes special problems for people dying of AIDS-related illnesses. Public health regulations require hospital staff to inform funeral directors, where someone has died of AIDS, that there is an 'infection risk'. There is no requirement that they specify a particular diagnosis.

Funeral directors' awareness of and prejudice about HIV/AIDS reflects that of the public and there is often an unnecessary caution. The Terrence Higgins Trust can provide information on undertakers with a sympathetic approach.

> *In general, those with more experience of HIV-related deaths are more likely to treat them like any other. However, it is not at all unusual, especially outside London, for undertakers to insist that the body goes into a heavy-duty plastic body bag which they do not permit to be reopened. They may also label the body and body bag and accompanying paperwork.*
>
> *If a body bag is to be used partners and friends need to be aware that they may not be allowed to see the body again, and any necessary religious rites should be performed first.*
>
> The Terrence Higgins Trust, *Death and Funerals*

There are only a handful of specialist AIDS hospices, all in the London area. Although there used to be difficulty in getting a place in a general hospice, the Hospice Information Service's *Directory '99* shows very few which are not willing to cater for someone with advanced AIDS.

There are other problems, especially for homosexual men, to do with the loss of their friends. As the HIV/AIDS epidemic has grown in Britain over the last dozen years, a major issue is emerging which is only now beginning to make itself felt – dealing with multiple bereavements. One of the aspects of bereavement is that it needs to be addressed at our own pace and we need time to become 'unhooked' from our attachment to someone. The effect of new bereavements coming before we have worked at the last can create a cumulative depression and confusion. In addition, the social stigma attached to AIDS and homosexuality often makes it harder to be open about our feelings and more difficult for others to attend to our grief.

The American homosexual community invented a memorial to AIDS victims in the form of a giant AIDS Quilt that toured different cities. There now exists a British version that is known as the Names Project. This is an enormous quilt that assembles 4,000 fabric panels in memory of individuals who have died. These panels are created by friends, partners and relatives: sometimes people with AIDS make their own before their death. For further information contact:

◆ The Names Project, c/o Crusaid, 25 Queensferry Street, Edinburgh EH2 4QS. Tel: (0131) 225 8982.

Further information about matters to do with HIV/AIDS can be obtained from:

◆ The Terrence Higgins Trust, 52–54 Gray's Inn Road, London WC1X 8JU. Tel: (020) 7831 0330.
◆ The National AIDS Helpline. Tel: 0800 567123. 24 hours and free.

Burial at sea

The waters were his winding sheet, the sea was made for his tomb,
Yet for his fame the ocean sea, was not sufficient room.

Richard Barnfield, *Epitaph on Hawkins,* 1595

Many people are drawn to the idea of being buried at sea either because of some previous marine connection or for the romance of it. Many people might think it is a 'cleaner' form of disposal than earth burial.

There are only about 20 such burials every year. This is not surprising considering how difficult it is to organise.

The first step is to tell the Registrar when you are registering the death. He will give you a 'Coroner's Out of England Form' which you should complete and send to the Coroner. Then you need to contact the Fishery Inspection Department at the Ministry of Agriculture, Fisheries and Food (MAFF) (Tel: (020) 7238 5872) to get a free licence. You also need a Freedom From Infection Certificate from a doctor.

Then you proceed with the burial. You are, however, only allowed to use two sites – one near Newhaven in East Sussex and the other near the Needles on the Isle of Wight. These are carefully selected tidally and away from trawler routes, which might disturb the grave.

There are marine companies that can organise the whole thing – for a price – including the collection of the body from anywhere in the country: MAFF can give you further details. Or you can organise it yourself – if you follow certain requirements:

◆ The coffin should not be made of any synthetic material or of wood which is sturdy enough to endure a long time in the water – use softwood such as pine. It will need to be large and stoutly built, with reinforced corners.

◆ There should be no non-ferrous metal involved – zinc, copper or lead.

◆ The coffin needs to be weighted with at least three hundredweight of steel or iron chain.

◆ At least 24 holes (2 cm in diameter) should be drilled in the sides and lid of the coffin to let in the water.

◆ The body should also be bound in heavy chains – to increase body weight by one-tenth.

◆ The body may not be embalmed. It is recommended that no canvas shroud is used: the body may be dressed, and wrapped in a sheet.

◆ There should be clear and permanent details of the

deceased, next of kin and date of the burial: this could be on a plastic label tied round the ankle.

◆ The Ministry should be informed the day before the burial and the day after it. An inspector has the right to make any checks.

Bodies immersed in water decompose nearly four times faster than in earth: if the water is warm or polluted it can be even quicker. However, if the water temperature is consistently cold there can be chemical changes in the body tissue which change it into 'adipocere' which is resistant to bacterial activity: this may well mean that there is some long-term preservation potential – all things being equal.

But all things are not equal. The effect of immersion in water causes body tissue to become white, soft, swollen and wrinkly – called 'washerwoman skin' by pathologists. It will quickly become loose and prey to aquatic insects and other marine life. Embalmed bodies, however, (which as you can see above are disallowed by MAFF) give off such toxic signals that fish will generally avoid them. Nevertheless, our internal bacteria and the physical effect of the water will do the job just as efficiently.

Eventually the body will decompose completely and return to the environment.

Pets and death

One of the most underestimated forms of bereavement is when someone loses a much-loved pet. We saw earlier that the depth of loss in a relationship is in proportion to the strength of the attachment. Many pet owners – particularly older, housebound people – are devoted to their cats, dogs and other animals. When the pet dies, others may regard their grief lightly and they often get little of the support given after human deaths. We may think such relationships are over-indulgent, but we mustn't deny the sense of loss and loneliness there can be.

As people get older and more alone they may hold back from owning a pet as they worry about what will happen to the animal if they should die before it. This can be a severe self-deprivation as research has shown the communicative and tactile importance of an attentive pet for people deprived of social and family contact.

Many animal shelters will come to an arrangement to take pets when their owners die and it is worth enquiring locally. One organisation that recognises this need is Wood Green Animal Shelters. They have a Pet Alert Scheme for pet owners. Members of the scheme are sent a set of cards with a contact number for the person who is entrusted with the immediate care of their pet if they should die or the need arise for some other reason. Their registration is logged on computer.

More often than not the service is unused because other arrangements are made with friends or family when the owner dies. However, the main value is the sense of reassurance the arrangement brings to someone anxious about the future. The scheme even organises the collection of 'bereaved' pets, although very long distances may be difficult and not in the best health interests of a grieving animal.

Wood Green Animal Shelters is a charity and whilst there is no expectation that anyone without means should make any financial provision, people who are able will wish to make some contribution to the scheme – perhaps through their will.

Amazingly, nearly all the pets involved are re-homed within a few weeks – even older animals. For more information contact:

◆ Wood Green Animal Shelters, King's Bush Farm, London Road, Godmanchester, Cambridgeshire PE18 8LJ. Tel: (01480) 830014. Fax: (01480) 830158.

Best behaviour

Werther had a love for Charlotte
Such as words could never utter;
Would you know how first he met her?
She was cutting bread and butter.

Charlotte was a married lady,
And a moral man was Werther,
And for all the wealth of Indes,
Would do nothing for to hurt her.

So he sighed and pined and ogled,
And his passion boiled and bubbled,
Till he blew his silly brains out,
And no more was by it troubled.

Charlotte, having seen his body
Borne before her on a shutter,
Like a well-conducted person,
Went on cutting bread and butter.

William Makepeace Thackeray, 'The Sorrows of Werther'

In the past there were elaborate customs – bird cages, mirrors
and indoor plants might be draped in black; in other parts of
Europe domestic animals had to be told of a family death and
the cat might be given a crepe collar; the trees might need to
be informed and dressed in mourning.

Thomas Lambton

Although I have been encouraging readers to be imaginative in
how they organise their own and others' funerals, there is
something to be said for the traditional funeral. Many people
will take comfort from familiar rituals, customs, ceremonies
and language. Their grief may be so keen that they need to
retreat for a while behind the known and well-established
processes that follow death – the quiet, the restraint, the
sadness, the funeral director, the church.

The Victorians had famously strict social regulations about
mourning dress and behaviour. More recently there were strict
customs about drawing front-room curtains, doffing your hat to
passing hearses and social codes for funerals. Nowadays there is
an embarrassed relaxation of the 'rules' which often leaves us
sometimes socially at a loss to know how best to behave when
faced with death and a funeral to attend.

Whether or not we have a religious belief we have come to
be comfortable with the traditional 'churchification' of funerals
– it is the way things have always been done, and is all the
more welcome in its familiarity. If some of us atheists want to
choose this tradition for ourselves or loved ones we are not
being hypocritical – we are doing what we feel is 'right'.

I am enthusiastic about alternative, secular ways of

arranging funerals and celebrating the lives of the dead. However, we must recognise the rights of others to have their own beliefs and organise things the way they wish. We ought therefore to have respect for and knowledge of the traditionally agreed rules and etiquette that relate to death and funerals.

There is a lot less to know than in Victorian times when the lives of bereaved people were dominated for months with subtleties to do with dress, relationships, social life and behaviour. Much of this obsessiveness was swept away during the 1914–18 war when people just couldn't keep pace with the millions of lost lives. Nowadays, there are few strict rules but there are ways of behaving which will be appreciated by many people:

◆ A member of the family should inform all other family members, friends and colleagues immediately of the death. This is to prevent them learning indirectly from a third party.

◆ Others can be informed by a simple letter announcing funeral arrangements: you can also indicate any other immediate requests:
'No flowers please, but donations to ...'
'Family flowers only....'
'No letters please ...'
'I would be pleased if you and Alan would join us here after the service for refreshments...'

◆ Everyone informed – by phone or letter – should send an immediate letter of sympathy (unless discouraged). We don't write many letters these days but these are usually valued.
Don't say: 'Let me know if there is anything I can do.'
Do say: 'Can I help organise the refreshments?
'Let me know if we can help by picking people up at the station.'
'I'll ring Mary in a few days time about what you would like me to do to help.'

◆ An alternative (or addition) to writing individually is to put a death announcement in the local newspaper:

ROBINSON – On May 9th at home, Christopher Percival

*Robinson, dearly loved husband of Catherine and father to
Susan, aged 73 years. Funeral service at Roundhill
Crematorium, Standerton on May 13th at 11 am. No flowers
please: donation to Friends of St John's Hospice, Holly Road,
Standerton.*

◆ All letters of sympathy should be promptly acknowledged.
These needn't be personalised replies – a standard format
will do. There may well be many – perhaps this could be
delegated.

*Jane has asked me to write to you to thank you for your kind
words of sympathy at this sad time. She and the family would
be pleased if you were able to attend the funeral at St Marks
Church next Tuesday at 11 am, although they would
understand if the short notice prevents this.*
   Jane will write personally to you at a later date.

◆ Take advantage of any offers of help. It is likely that they
are genuinely intended.
◆ If people wish to send flowers they should be sent to the
funeral director the day before the funeral. Flowers are a
tribute to the deceased and should be addressed to them:
'For Robert. In fond memory. ' They are not meant to
express sympathy for the survivors. By all means send some
flowers to the widow, but leave it a day or two.
◆ The family usually congregate at the home of the deceased
immediately before the funeral. The hearse and limousine
arrive with the coffin (or the coffin is moved out of the
house). Members of the immediate family occupy the
funeral car and others follow in procession.
◆ A member of the family or a friend will have been at the
church or crematorium to greet other members of the
congregation, who will be seated inside. The family are the
last to arrive. Seats will have been reserved for them at the
front.
◆ If there is a burial in the churchyard or cemetery it is
attended only by the principal mourners, unless others are
specifically invited.
◆ It is no longer necessary for clothing to be black, although

many people will feel that it is more appropriate and comfortable to wear sombre colours.

◆ Showy jewellery should be avoided in keeping with the general restraint. This restraint should not be expected from the immediate family who should feel free to express their sense of loss.

In conclusion

When I began researching this book, I was apprehensive. Like most people I had a rough idea of the subject, but I was aware that there was much material which could be potentially challenging. I would be facing up to my own feelings about my own death.

Many of us have a jumbled concept of death which includes worms, heaven, fear, judgement, weeping and solemnity: there is a feeling that if we look more closely we will only find more (and worse) of the same.

I realised that in the course of my research, I would be learning exactly what will happen to me as I die and what people will do to my body. I would be visiting cemeteries, crematoria and funeral directors. I would be reading things on the Internet that should only be seen with parental guidance.

The curious thing is that the more I have learned, the more settled I have become in my mind about the prospect of my death. It is not that I have become more philosophical or achieved a deeper level of wisdom. I have not become wiser or more psychologically mature. I just know much more than I did.

In the same way that I feel comfortable about the geographical nooks and crannies of my home town after years of familiarity, I feel after the months spent researching this book that there remains little I don't know about dying and death (of the things that are able to be known). It's not hard to gain such knowledge: it's simply a matter of interest, time and persistence.

I now know what will happen to my body from now, through old age and up to the time it will have become particles of dust or ash. It won't be a pretty sight. But knowing the facts and removing the uncertainties brings with it a certain comfort and settlement of anxieties.

I am also clearer about things I can do whilst I am alive to add to the fullness of my remaining years and give greater support to my survivors.

More importantly, I have come to grasp some of the roots of our fears and horror of losing our lives and being abandoned by the death of those we love.

Earlier I referred to the central issues of attachment and loss. Learning to 'look after' our attachments and understand our sense of loss seems to me most important if we wish to have mature relationships and a life which is not constantly under the cloud of impending death.

Things start innocently enough. Our parents feed our infant sense of self-importance and encourage our power to achieve. Education and careers are built on competition to gain certificates, promotion and security. We value people who achieve and we disapprove of people who lack ambition:

Good things		Bad things	
growth	progress	passivity	acceptance
aspirations	competition	indecision	uncertainty
power	ownership	humility	forbearance
prosperity	advancement	stoicism	indifference

Our existence is based on the continual *expansion* of our lives by packing in as many of the 'good' things. People who show signs of the 'bad' tendencies we regard as 'not having made much of their lives.'

The 'good people' hit life running. They have:

◆ the excitement of the chase
◆ the pride of the victor
◆ the power to change things
◆ the power to direct other people
◆ the respect of their rivals
◆ the praise of their peers
◆ honours from the State.

Their (our?) lives are shaped by this constant need for improvement. This is not a context where death can play *any* useful part at all. It becomes the most feared enemy in the world.

Being able to accept death and look it in the eye from a distance means that we need to modify our priorities. We need to ask ourselves whether the rewards of the 'good' life – excitement, pride, power, respect, praise and honours – are sufficiently 'grown up' for mature adults to make sense of the jigsaw where room needs to be found for the final piece: death.

Only by living our lives modestly in the present and facing the fact that ultimately our real and only satisfactions come from what we do and have today, will we be able to become indifferent to death.

One of the early lessons we learn in life is usually 'to do things properly':

> *'If at first you don't succeed...'*
> *'If a job's worth doing...'*
> *'See it through to the end.'*

We grasp the concept of perfection early on and our success in life is measured in terms of how closely we come near it. We prefer 'whole' and 'complete' to 'partial' and 'unfinished'.

One of the things that we can always say about someone's life is that it was incomplete: nearly complete, maybe, but never wholly so – death sees to that. We strive to complete our education, our work competence; we develop mature relationships.

The first big step towards completing our life comes with the birth of our children. We hold our breath through their childhood (death quite likes young children). We can begin to relax when they become adults and have children of their own: we can be pretty sure then that we have been survived.

However, all the while we know that unexpected death stands in the wings to ruin all our plans. Mostly we succeed in wishing it away for a few decades. However, by middle age our place on the stage at work and in the family is taken over by our successors. For many people this means that they no longer have a job or family to complete: all that's left is the approaching, beckoning figure of death.

The trick is not to have anything to do with a 'working life' or a 'job as a mother' because these will inevitably come to an end. We should organise things so that we can look forward to similarly satisfying occupations when our employment ends or the family leave home.

The biggest attachment most of us have is with our partners and friends: the loss of someone after many years of intimacy can be the cause of the greatest distress of our lives. But it does not have to be so. We can have deeper, freer relationships with our partners if we are able to have direct, unconditional, non-manipulative communication with them. Can we relate to them for who they are today rather than because of who they were in the past or who they might be in the future?

◆ Is the relationship free of power and control?
◆ Is there any unexpressed guilt?
◆ How dependent, emotionally and practically, are we on each other?

Many people see *dependence, being in charge, being submissive* or *being strong* as tokens of love: many relationships exist in a web of power, domination, fear and long-suffering. If we are locked into such relationships, the death of a partner will leave us bereft. The person who defined our identity has gone and left us – stage-frightened – alone in the theatre.

'Healthy' attachments are not less close. We can pleasurably allow someone to play a complementary role in our life without becoming disabled. We can spread our interests in life so that our whole existence does not revolve around our partner. It is not that we love them less: it's a question of showing respect for their – and our individuality.

Finally, I have learned the value of getting things into proportion. On the whole we take things too seriously. We have an inflated sense of our own importance: we either overestimate our influence on events or we beat our breasts about our 'unfulfilled' lives. We have this curiously 'immature' need to live on through our children.

We spend massive amounts of time, energy and money worrying about the postponement of death so that we can have more time to worry about dying.

It is only through letting go of our pride, arrogance and

anxiety that we can learn to live to appreciate the present moment: to relish the good things of life – other people, personal skills, creativity, the natural world, art, literature.... Death will come in due course, but Life is more interesting at the moment.

> *The present life of man on earth is like the flight of a single sparrow through the hall where, in winter, you sit with your captains and ministers. Entering at one door and leaving by another, whilst it is inside it is untouched by the wintry storm: but this brief interval of calm is over in a moment, and it returns to the winter whence it came, vanishing from your sight. Man's life is similar: and of what follows it, or what went before, we are utterly ignorant.*
>
> The Venerable Bede (672–735)

CHAPTER 10

Telegrams from the Grave

*REGRET TO INFORM YOU. HAND THAT ROCKED THE
CRADLE KICKED THE BUCKET.*

Anonymous telegram 1993

Epitaphs and death wisdom

*In memory of Mary, wife of James Pink.
For nearly 50 years the faithful servant of MRS GRIMES.
This stone is affectionately raised.*

19th C. memorial, Isle of Wight

What hopes lie buried here.

Early American epitaph

*Beneath this stone, in hope of Zion,
Doth lie the landlord of the 'Lion'.
His son keeps on the business still,
Resigned unto the Heavenly will.*

Epitaph, Upton-on-Severn

*Here lies a wife
Of two husbands bereft:
Robert on the right,
Richard on the left.*

Early American epitaph

*Mary Nichols is my name,
Ireland is my nation,
The Catholic Church is my belief,
Heaven is my expectation.*

Epitaph, New Orleans cemetery

Here lies a poor woman who always was tired,
For she lived in a place where help wasn't hired.
Her last words on earth were, 'Dear friends I am going
Where washing ain't done nor sweeping nor sewing.
And everything there is exact to my wishes,
For there they don't eat and there's no washing of dishes.
Don't mourn for me now, don't mourn for me never,
For I'm going to do nothing forever and ever.'

Epitaph, Bushey 1860

Here lies Jan Smith, wife of Thomas Smith, marble cutter.
This monument was erected by her husband as a tribute to
her memory and a specimen of his work.
(Monuments of the same style 350 dollars).

Memorial in an Ohio churchyard

Sixteen years a Maiden
One twelve month a Wife,
One half hour a Mother,
And then I lost my Life.

Epitaph, Folkestone

Here lies the body of Richard Hind
Who was neither ingenious, sober or kind.

Memorial in an Ohio churchyard

He lived a life of going-to-do
And died with nothing done.

James Albery, on himself

Doctor, do you think it could have been the sausage?

Paul Claudel, 1955

Erected to the memory of
John MacFarlane
Drown'd in the Water of Leith
By a few affectionate friends

Memorial in an Edinburgh churchyard

The silver swan, who, living, had no note,
When death approached unlocked her silent throat;
Leaning her breast against the reedy shore,
Thus sung her first and last, and sung no more:
'Farewell all joys; O death, come close mine eyes;
More geese than swans now live, more fools than wise.'

Orlando Gibbons, 'The Silver Swan', 1610

Underneath this pile of stones
Lies all that's left of Sally Jones.
Her name was Briggs: it was not Jones
But Jones was used to rhyme with stones

Memorial in a New York churchyard

All who come my grave to see,
Avoid damp beds and think of me.

Epitaph, Stoke-on-Trent

Poorly lived,
And poorly died,
Poorly buried,
And nobody cried.

Epitaph, Lillington

WE	MUST	ALL	DIE
MUST	WE	DIE	ALL
ALL	DIE	WE	MUST
DIE	ALL	MUST	WE

Memorial, Bacton, Norfolk

My wife she's dead, and here she lies,
There's nobody laughs, and nobody cries:
Where she's gone, and how she fares
Nobody knows, and nobody cares.

Epitaph, Stepney churchyard

As I am now, so you must be:
Therefore prepare to follow me.

Memorial, Woolwich Churchyard

To follow you I'm not content
Until I know which way you went.

Scrawled on the above memorial

Death, in itself, is nothing: but we fear
To be we know not what, we know not where.

John Dryden (1631–1700)

Our repugnance to death increases in proportion to our
consciousness of having lived in vain.

Hazlitt, *On the Love of Life*, 1815

There is no cure for birth and death save to enjoy the interval.

George Santayana

Death is more universal than life; everyone dies but not
everyone lives.

A. Sachs

Life is better than death, I believe, if only because it is less
boring, and because it has fresh peaches in it.

Alice Walker

Death is not the greatest loss in life. The greatest loss is what
dies inside us while we live.

Norman Cousins

The average man, who doesn't know what to do with his life,
wants another one, which will last forever.

Anatole France

Many people's tombstones should read, Died at 30; buried at
60.

Nicholas Murray Butler

While I thought that I was learning how to live,
I have been learning how to die.

Leonardo da Vinci

Death is nothing to us, since when we are, death has not
come, and when death has come, we are not.

Epicurus, *Diogenes Laertius*

Life does not cease to be funny when people die any more
than it ceases to be serious when people laugh.

George Bernard Shaw

We are each in a plane that will finally crash into a
mountainside one day. Most people forget this. I think about it
every day. But, perhaps that's because I can begin to catch a
glimpse of the mountain out of the window.

François Mitterand

I don't want to achieve immortality through my work, I want
to achieve it through not dying.

Woody Allen

You can keep the things of bronze and stone and give me one
man to remember me just once a year.

Damon Runyon, last words

Nothing speaks our grief so well
As to speak nothing.

Richard Crashaw, '1646'

Those who have known grief seldom seem sad.

Benjamin Disraeli, *Endymion*, 1880

A good occasion for courtship is
When the widow returns from the funeral.

H. G. Bohn, *Handbook of Proverbs*

Appendix I
Public Opinion About Assisted Death

British Social Attitudes: the 13th Report (1996) shows increasing public acknowledgement for some clarification in the law: the same question was asked three times over ten years:

'Suppose a person has a painful, incurable disease. Do you think that doctors should be allowed by law to end the patient's life, if the person requests it?'

These are the responses:

	1984	1989	1994
The law should allow it	*75 per cent*	*79 per cent*	*82 per cent*
The law should not allow it	*24 per cent*	*20 per cent*	*15 per cent*

It's surprising that only a couple of people in every hundred reveal any uncertainty in the matter. There is, however, a variation in people's attitudes when different situations are proposed:

'The percentage of people who think euthanasia should 'definitely' or 'probably' be allowed by law for a person...'

> *...who has an incurable illness which leaves them unable to make a decision about their own future. For instance, imagine a person in a coma on a life support machine who is never expected to regain consciousness (if their relatives agree).*
>
> 86 per cent

> *...who has an incurable and painful illness from which they will die. For example, someone dying of cancer.*
>
> 80 per cent

... in a coma. never expected to regain consciousness, but is not on a life support machine (if their relatives agree).

85 per cent

... who is not in much pain, nor in danger of death, but becomes permanently and completely dependent on relatives for all their needs. For example, someone who cannot feed, wash or go to the toilet by themselves.

51 per cent

... with an incurable disease from which they will die, but is not in very much pain – as might be the case of someone suffering from leukaemia.

44 per cent

... with an incurable and painful illness from which they will not die. For example, someone with severe arthritis.

42 per cent

... who is not ill or close to death, but who is simply tired of living and wishes to die – for example, someone who is extremely lonely and no longer enjoys life.

12 per cent

(Source: *British Social Attitudes: the 13th Report* 1996)

Appendix II
Laying-Out a Body

- Remove sheets and blankets from the bed; put a cover on the bed with a plastic undersheet.
- Lay the body flat with the limbs straight. Support the head with a small pillow.
- Remove all clothing.
- Close the eyelids gently with the palm of the hand or fingers.
- The absence of muscle tension may mean that the jaw has dropped open. Close it by looping a scarf underneath and secure it gently at the top of the head or support the chin on a small pillow. Before closing the mouth it should be washed inside and any dentures replaced or the natural teeth cleaned.
- Fluids from within the body may begin to leak out if the other orifices are not secured: to do this you should plug the nostrils, throat, vagina and anus with cotton wool. Use an incontinence pad, if available, for both sexes.
- There may be some urine retained in the bladder: by pressing gently on the lower abdomen it can be expelled on to a towel (or use an incontinence pad).
- Remove any intravenous needles or drainage tubes and cover any holes or pastures with waterproof tape.
- The body should be washed and cleaned with a disinfectant spray: front first, including the face – not forgetting the mouth, nostrils, and ears. The back is then washed and any bedsores covered with waterproof tape.
- Hair should be combed and a man's face shaved (if he was clean-shaven.)
- Nails should be cleaned and trimmed.
- If the bottom sheet is soiled, replace it.
- This is the best time to dress the body for the final time.

Appendix III
Funeral Costs by UK Region

The average costs across Britain for a funeral were surveyed recently. The costs in the table below are average charges for basic funerals, including disbursements. As you can see, there are wide geographical variations. If you want an elaborate coffin, more cars or a headstone, you'll pay more.

	Burial £	Cremation £
National average	1,657	1,101
London	2,391	1,302
Rest of South East	1,429	1,020
Scotland	1,912	1,131
Wales	1,300	1,004
Channel Isles	1,572	1,222
South West	1,402	915
East Anglia	1,503	931
East Midlands	1,269	912
West Midlands	1,620	935
Yorkshire and Humberside	1,632	1,195
North West	1,737	1,292
North	1,823	1,308

Quoted in *The Guardian*, October 1998

Appendix IV
Checklist of Things to be Done after a Death

This is not a complete list covering everyone's individual circumstances. You should return the following, with a note of explanation and the date of death with each of the items:

◆ The deceased's passport to the Passport Office. You can get the address from a post offiice.

◆ Order books, payable orders or girocheques to the Social Security office or other office which issued the payment. This applies also to a Child Benefit book that includes payment for a child who has died. Orders should not be cashed after the death of the person. It may be useful to keep a record of pension book numbers or other Social Security numbers before you send anything back.

◆ The deceased's driving license to DVLA, Longview Road, Swansea SA6 7JL.

◆ The registration document of a car, for the change of ownership to be recorded.

◆ Any season tickets. Claim any refund due.

◆ Membership cards of clubs and associations. Claim any refund due.

◆ Library books and tickets.

◆ Any National Insurance papers to the relevant office.

◆ Any equipment such as wheelchairs, hearing aids, artificial limbs should be returned.

People to tell

You should tell:

◆ The offices of the local electricity, gas or telephone company.

◆ The local social services department of the council if the person was getting meals-on-wheels, home help or day-centre care or had an appliance or piece of equipment issued by the department.

◆ Any hospital the person was attending.

◆ The family doctor to cancel any home nursing.

◆ The Inland Revenue.

◆ The Benefits Agency if money was being paid directly into a bank or building society account; for example, Retirement Pension, Attendance Allowance.

◆ Any employer and trade union.

◆ A child or young person's teacher; employer or college if a parent, brother, sister, grandparent or close friend has died.

◆ The car insurance company (if you are insured to drive the car under the deceased's name, you will cease to be legally insured).

◆ The local council housing department if the person who has died was living in a council house.

◆ The local council Housing Benefit/Council Tax Benefit section if the person who has died was getting Housing Benefit and/or Council Tax Benefit.

◆ The Post office so that they can redirect mail.

Appendix V
Making Your Own Coffin

People with even basic carpentry skills are able to make a coffin: a couple of sheets of chipboard or blockboard, some strengthening battens, wood-glue and screws. There's no need for the characteristic coffin shape: just make a long rectangular box. One way of doing it is to make it as an upright bookcase or storage cabinet: when the time comes the shelves can be removed.

If you do make your own coffin, you should be aware that there are regulations about its construction if it is going to be cremated:

◆ The coffin for cremation should be made of wood or wood by-product (e.g. an approved cardboard coffin) which when placed in a cremator is easily combusted and which does not emit smoke, give off toxic gas or leave any retardant smears or drips after final combustion....

◆ A suitable nameplate, indicating the name and age of the deceased, must be affixed to the lid of the coffin.

◆ If handles are to be fitted to the sides of the coffin these must be securely fixed. No metal fittings whatever should be used on a coffin for cremation.

◆ No metal of any kind should be used in the manufacture of the coffin except as necessary for safe construction, and then only metal of a high ferrous content.

◆ Crosspieces should not be attached to the bottom of the coffin. If it is desired to strengthen the bottom, wooden strips may be placed lengthways for this purpose.

◆ The coffin should not be painted or varnished but may be covered in a suitable cloth.

◆ Products in polyvinyl chloride (PVC) must not be used in the construction of the coffin or its furnishings. The use of polystyrene should be restricted to the coffin nameplate only.

◆ There are also restrictions on dress applicable to the deceased, e.g. no shoes or teddy bears (for environmental reasons). The use of sawdust or cotton wool in the lining of the coffin should be avoided. If circumstances require, suitable sealing material may be used, but no metal, rubber or polyvinyl/chloride (PVC) will be permitted and on no account must pitch or similar substances be used.
◆ No lead-lined coffins will be permitted.

(Publicity from Emstrey Crematorium, Shropshire)

The sensible thing is to consult your crematorium if you plan to use anything other than natural wood panels, battens and a few steel wood-screws.

Appendix VI
Further Reading

To Have or to Be, Eric Fromm, The Aquarian Press 1979.
How We Die, Sherwin B. Nuland, Chatto & Windus 1994.
The Hour of our Death, Phillipe Aries, Editions de Seuil 1973.
Merely Mortal, Sarah Boston and Rachael Trezise, Methuen 1988.
The Natural Death Handbook, Nicholas Albery, The Natural Death Centre 1998.
Causing Death and Saving Lives, Jonathan Glover.
Funerals Without God, Jane Wynne Willson, British Humanist Association 1989.
Green Burial, J. B. Bradfield, Natural Death Centre 1994.
When We Die, Cedric Mims, Robinson 1998.
Concise Guide to Customs of Minority Ethnic Religions, David Collins, Arena 1993.
The Tasks of Grieving, Dr Tony Lake, Sheldon Press 1988.
Living with Grief, Tony Lake, Sheldon Press 1984.
Funerals and How To Improve Them, Tony Walter, Hodder & Stoughton 1990.
Intimate Death, Marie de Hennezel, Warner Books 1995.
Death, Dying and Bereavement, Dickenson & Johnson: Sage Publications 1996.
A Grief Observed, C. S. Lewis, Faber & Faber, 1966.
What To Do After A Death, Department of Social Security Leaflet D49, DSS Leaflets Unit, PO Box 21, Stanmore, Middx HA7 1AY.
The Prophet, Kahlil Gibran, Arkana Press 1926.
The Good Death, Michael Young and Lesley Cullen, Routledge 1996.
A Good Age, Alex Comfort, Mitchell Beazley 1977.

Appendix VII
Death on the Internet

Death, dying and grief resources: these are large websites which will provide links to most other sites of interests.

Hospice organisations in the UK and Ireland

http://www.hauraki.co.uk/hospice_uk
An up-to-date list of hospice information pages on the internet.

Bacup

http://medweb.bham.ac.uk/cancerhelp/public/bacup/
Support for people with cancer and their families and friends.

GriefNet

http://griefnet.org/
'This award-winning website is your international gateway to resources for life-threatening illness and end-of-life care. Our primary mission is to improve the quality of compassionate care for people who are dying through public education and global professional collaboration.'

Webster's Guide to Death and Dying

www.katsden.com/death
'This web site represents a large and comprehensive collection of Internet resources with a holistic perspective – one that would be helpful to anyone seeking a wider vision and understanding of the death process. It is focused on death as "natural" and expected for all living beings.'

City 2000 Legal Information Service

http://www.city2000.com/legal/info/wills.html

Information about making wills.

The Desktop Lawyer

http://www desktoplawyer.freeserve.net/law/
Legal information: wills: living wills. You can download sample
proformas for doing it yourself.

Widow Net

http://www.fortnet.org/WidowNet/
This is a resource for widows and widowers, and is based in the
USA. The book list is good, particularly as it includes
suggestions for reading from those who have been bereaved.
There is an email service, which can get you in touch with
others; you can expect about 60–100 notes a day.

London Association of Bereavement Services

http://www.bereavement.demon.co.uk
'LABS has a good list of links to resources for the bereaved.
Particularly noteworthy is its list of sites for people of different
cultural backgrounds and religions.'

SIDS (Sudden Infant Death Syndrome) Network

http://sids-network.org/
Many more children die of SIDS in a year than all who die of
cancer, heart disease, pneumonia, child abuse, AIDS, cystic
fibrosis and muscular dystrophy combined. This site is the
growing collaborative effort of individuals from across the
United States and around the world. This site offers up-to-date
information as well as support for those who have been
touched by the tragedy of SIDS. This site not only deals with
stillbirth and neonatal death, but also issues such as sibling
grief. Most of the links are to other sites in the USA.

Kearl's Guide to the Sociology of Death

http://www.trinity.edu/~mkearl/death.html
'Unlike many of the more psychologically-oriented pages here

in cyberspace, the orientation here is sociological. It is here assumed that individuals' fears of death and experiences of dying and grief are not innate but rather are shaped by social environments. This site has interesting and objective information on homicide and suicide. The section dealing with the personal impact of death deals with the loss of a child, widowhood and grief. The list of links to other sites is good.'

Natural Death Centre

http://www.worldtrans.org/naturaldeath.html
A fascinating website which looks at death impassionately. It is particularly strong on resources for alternative funerals. There is a link which gives access to the complete text of the 1994 edition of the *Natural Death Handbook*. A must.

A Virtual Garden of Remembrance

www.cemetery.org/
'Monuments in the World Wide Cemetery allow people to share the lives of their loved ones in ways that traditional printed death announcements or stone inscriptions cannot. Photographs, moving images and even sounds can be included with a monument. People can create hypertext links among family members, and in doing so forge a genealogy of Internet users and their families online and in real time.'

The Loved Ones

www.TheLovedOnes.com
'The first serious attempt of a British company to offer a long-lasting and professional virtual memorial facility on the Internet (£8.00 a year for a minimum of five years.)

The DeathClock

www.deathclock.com
You can find out your deathday (as well as other matters of interest).

How Long Will You Live Really?

http://www.msnbc.com/modules/quizzes/lifex.asp
A more sophisticated calculator of remaining mortality.

Index

accidental death, 89, 115
advance directives, 68
ageing process, 7
alcohol, 33
algormortis, 105
Alzheimer's disease, 36, 50, 56, 72, 95
anticipated death, 72
arranging a funeral, 119
assertiveness, 59
assisted death, 93, 221
asthma, 13, 56
atherosclerosis, 8
attachment, 177

basic funeral, 122
Belgium, 64, 142
Benefits Agency, 12
bereavement, 176
Bereavement Benefits, 153
biological perspective, 5
bladders, 10
body donation, 67
brains, 10
brainstem death, 66, 99
brain stem test, 66, 101
breast cancer, 36
breathlessness, 20
British Humanists' Society, 72, 168
bronchitis, 12
burial
    at sea, 204
    booking, 161
    churchyard, 140
    cemeteries, 139

club, 23
woodland, 165

cancer, 12, 38, 56, 58
calories, 53
cardiovascular disease, 36
Carlisle Bereavement Service, 124
Cause of Death Certificate, 111
causes of death, 35
Cecily Saunders, 90
cemeteries, 139
centenarians, 29
cigarettes, 33
cirrhosis of liver, 12
Chapel of Remembrance, 145
cholera, 111
claims on the estate, 150
constipation, 20
Church Commissioners, 126
coffins
    acquiring, 157
    cardboard, 159
    carrying, 162
    making your own, 227
    suppliers, 158
    transporting, 161
Compakta, 159
Co-operative Funeral Service, 120
coronary artery disease, 52
coroner, 114
counselling, 77
cremains, 144
cremation, 113, 141, 161
cremators, 142, 145

crypthanasia, 103

Dawkins, Richard, 2
death rate, 23
deaths
  babies, 196
  children, 193
  in other cultures, 200
  parents, 191
decomposition processes, 107
dental health, 34
dehydration, 102
depression, 34
determination, 55
diabetes, 13, 31, 56
diet, 33, 59
digestive system, 49
Diploma in Funeral Directing, 123
disbursements, 126
DNA material, 40
drugs, 34

ecological argument, 4
education, 59
Elizabeth Kubler-Ross, 82, 176
embalming, 108, 133
emphysema, 13, 56
Enduring Power of Attorney, 71
etiquette, 208
estate, sorting out the, 148
euphemisms, 27
euthanasia, 93, 221
executor, 148
exercise, 32, 34, 47, 54

family, 32
fatal accident enquiry, 115
fear of dying, 14
fight or flight, 49
flowers, 210
funeral

complaints, 133
costs, 124
costs by UK region, 224
director, 119
gathering, 162
ombudsman, 133

garlic, 46
gender differences, 37
ginseng, 46
graves, 139
gravestones, 147
grief
  help, 187
  injuries, 185
  opportunities, 186

Health Authority, 128
hearing, 7
heart disease, 9, 12, 31
hearts, 9
Heaven on Earth, 158
helping bereaved people, 187
Hindu religion, 145
HIV/AIDS, 66, 72, 111, 202
Holland, 97
homosexuality, 75, 201
home burials, 164
home organised funerals, 154
Hospice Information Service, 92
hospice movement, 89
hospital, dying in, 25
Huntingdon's Chorea, 36

Income Support, 152
imagination, 50
immortality, 40
immune system, 11
inheritance, 61
Inheritance tax, 63, 150
inquest, 115

intelligence, 33
internet memorials, 147
internet addresses, 230
intestacy, 61
involuntary assisted death, 99

kidneys, 10, 49, 64

lack of appetite, 20
lactic acid, 107
language, 27, 78
laying out a body, 110, 223
letters of sympathy, 210
leukaemia, 38
London Zoo, 5
life expectancy, 29
lifespan, 53
lightning strikes, 38
liver, 49
living wills, 68
Local Authorities, 128
lungs, 9, 56

Macmillan nurses, 21, 92
Marie Curie Cancer Care, 21, 92
marriage, 32
mastectomies, 55
mausoleums, 141
meaning of life , 2
melanoma, 36
memes, 3
memorials, 147
menopause, 3
mental health, 52
miscarriage, 196
moderation, 48
mortuary, 156
mourning dress, 210
multiple sclerosis, 72
mummification, 107, 109
murder, 89

music, 170
Muslims, 21
National Association of Funeral
    Directors, 120, 121, 133
Natural Death Centre, 155
Natural Death Handbook, 155
nausea, 20
near death experience, 82, 105
NHS Organ Donor Register, 64

obituaries, 173
officiants, 126, 166, 168
opiates, 21
optimism, 48
Order for Cremation or burial, 115
organ donation, 64
osteoporosis, 54

pacemaker, 118, 160
pain, 19
painkillers, 20
palliative care, 21
pathologist, 116
paying for a funeral, 128
people to tell following a death, 225
persistent vegetative state, 99
pets and death, 206
plague, 111
pleasure, 48
pollution, 34, 58
poverty, 32, 57
post mortems, 116
pre-purchased funerals, 129
pride, 47
probate, 149
process of dying, 104
prognosis, 79
public health, 116
putrefaction, 107

refreshments, 210

registering the death, 111, 155
relapsing fever, 111
religion, 19, 43, 52
reproductive system, 11, 49
residential care, dying in, 26
respiratory disease, 12
rigor mortis, 107, 134

secular funeral, 165
self-confidence, 47
sense of humour, 48
Service Corporation International, 120,
  121, 140
sex, 34, 54
sleep, 34, 59
smallpox, 111
sociability, 47
social contact, 53
Social Fund Funeral Payment, 128
social inequality, 56, 58
social work, 26
Society of Allied and Independent
  Funeral Directors, 120, 122, 133
St Christopher's Hospice, 90
stillbirth, 196
storing the body, 156
stress, 33, 48
stroke, 12
sudden death, 88

suspicious circumstances, 116
suicide, 1, 89, 115, 197

Terrence Higgins Trust, 204
testosterone, 11
things to be done after a death, 226
thrombosis, 36
tolerance, 47
trocar, 135
typhus, 111
unfinished business, 73

vegetarianism, 46, 47
Victorians, 27
visual acuity, 7
Voluntary Euthanasia Society, 71
vomiting, 20

weight, 33
welfare benefits, 151
Widowed Mothers' Allowance, 152
Widows' payment, 151
willed fasting, 102
wills, 61
Wood Green Animal Shelters, 207
woodland burials, 165
world population, 5
Wrekin Funeral Services, 125
writing your own will, 62